In His Majesty's Service

Christians in Politics

by Robert A. Peterson

HUNTINGTON HOUSE PUBLISHERS

Huntington House Publishers
P.O. Box 53788
Lafayette, Louisiana 70505

Library of Congress Card Catalog Number 95-77217
ISBN 1-56384-100-2

Printed in the U.S.A.

Dedication

This book is dedicated to my parents,
Robert and Nancy Peterson, Sr.,
who first opened my eyes to history and
taught me what "family values" really mean.

Contents

Acknowledgments   vii

Introduction   ix

Chapter 1
Edward VI:
Good King Edward   13

Chapter 2
William Bradford:
The First American   25

Chapter 3
John Winthrop:
Governor of Massachusetts   43

Chapter 4
Nathaniel Ward:
Author of America's First Bill of Rights   63

Chapter 5
John Witherspoon:
Son of Liberty   73

Chapter 6
    Richard Bassett:
    Governor of Delaware   99

Chapter 7
    William Wilberforce:
    The Man Who Freed the Slaves   113

Chapter 8
    Sir Robert Anderson:
    Christian Civil Servant   133

Chapter 9
    Abraham Kuyper:
    Prime Minister of Holland   147

Chapter 10
    Conclusion   177

Notes   181

Acknowledgments

Without the help of the following individuals, this book would have been much longer in the making and, when finished, contain many more errors.

My college professors Dr. William Ketchersid and Dr. Robert Spoede laid an excellent foundation for all my subsequent research by emphasizing sound scholarship and good writing. (All our tests were essays.) Dr. E. William Male of Grace Theological Seminary gave numerous helpful suggestions and supported my Master's thesis on John Witherspoon (the subject of chapter 5). Dr. Warren Allem, founder and Headmaster Emeritus of The Pilgrim Academy, encouraged me to write and speak out on Christianity and politics.

Michael and Linda Ventura had enough faith in the manuscript to take it to Dr. Joseph Kickasola of Regent University, who made helpful suggestions and passed it on to Dr. Walter Davis, author of *History, Thought and Culture, 1600-1815* (Lanham: University Press of America). Dr. Davis did an excellent job of editing the manuscript. When I read his comments, I kept saying to myself, "I knew that." One of my History Seminar students, Daniel Hart, also read the manuscript and provided suggestions. Renatti Dupont, my sponsoring editor at Huntington House, has been helpful and patient.

Special thanks go to Lois Boone, my administrative assistant and secretary of thirteen years, who put the manuscript on computer, making corrections and suggestions as she worked. Without her help, this book would not be in print today. She was able to type the manuscript at a time when my wife and I were surrounded by a whirlwind of other responsibilities. Both she and her husband John are models of what Christian laymen can do and be, working quietly behind the scenes to advance the Gospel.

Finally, I'd like to thank my wife Susanna and children—Rebecca, Robert III, Joseph, James, David, Priscilla, and Rachel—for their patience in putting up with their husband-father-writer. Susanna, an English teacher, also typed the manuscript twice and offered many good suggestions. Someday, when I get my first million dollar advance, they are all in for a big treat.

Introduction

As this book goes to press, a controversy is raging in America—whether Christians should be involved in politics or not. The very fact that such a debate is going on at all shows how much of our heritage we have forgotten. At one time, not so long ago, Christians called the tune and everyone else danced (or didn't dance) to their music. As historian Louis B. Wright put it in *The Cultural Life of the American Colonies* (New York: Harper and Row, 1957), p. 72:

> When a dweller in the mid-twentieth century tries to project himself into the period of his colonial ancestors, one of his greatest difficulties is a comprehension of the pervasiveness of religion and its universal influence upon men, women, and children of the earlier age. Religious beliefs were almost as varied then as now; but whatever men believed, they believed with greater devotion than most of their descendants display today. That is not to say that our ancestors were more virtuous than we, but that they were more God-fearing. When the wicked sinned, more of them trembled in fear of eternal damnation.
>
> Religion was not merely a Sunday ritual; in the seventeenth century it was an enveloping influence seven days in the week, and its all-pervad-

ing vitality lasted throughout the colonial period and affected all shades of opinion; Puritan,
Anglican, Quaker, or Catholic.

So great was the Christian influence on early
America that when John Jay, our first Chief Justice,
suggested that only Christians be allowed to run for
office, no one questioned him or showed any alarm.
Similarly, when in 1832 a New York judge disqualified
a witness because he was an atheist, it was reported
without comment in the local paper.

The very success of Christians in politics is, in a
sense, part of our present problem. Because of Christian influence, the nation was singularly blessed. This,
coupled with America's victories in World War I and
II, put America on top of the world by the mid-twen-
tieth century. But, instead of acknowledging that their
blessings came from God and His principles, Americans attributed their successes to man's efforts—through
social engineering, through the power of the government, and so on. This heady attitude reached its zenith
under Lyndon Johnson, who thought that America's
wealth, coupled with the wisdom of government bu-
reaucrats, could wipe out poverty. Meanwhile, Bible
reading and prayer, even in their simplest forms, were
regarded as trivial and removed from the public schools.
As one wag put it, God was replaced by half a million
social workers.

But, by the late seventies, just a decade later, it was
clear that secularism was dead. There were, of course,
powerful forces—including billions of tax-dollars—keeping it on life support. (And so it continues today.) But,
as a valid philosophy of life or government, it was and
is an abject failure.

It was in the late seventies that I first got involved
in politics, immediately after graduating from college
and going to work in a Christian school. Like many

Christians, my concerns dealt mainly with family, the church, friends, work, and local ministries. But, when the IRS—with the blessing of the Carter Administration—launched a vindictive campaign against private Christian schools, I thought our government had become especially unfair. Here we were, minding our own business, teaching Christian morals and helping youth in a peaceful way, and now the country that my ancestors had fought and died for (and financed) for generations was trying to put us out of business. (The issue was quotas—ironically, we had a higher percentage of minority students than many public schools in our area.)

The IRS attack on Christian schools ultimately failed, but my interest in politics only grew. I joined the local Republican Club and became the legislative director for the Garden State Association of Christian Schools, the local chapter of the American Association of Christian Schools. Meanwhile, my research continued in American history and the role that religion played in shaping the Western world. My mentors in those years (through their books and articles) were men like Dr. Rousas Rushdoony of the Chalcedon Foundation, Dr. Francis Schaeffer of L'Abri, Dr. Paul Kienel of the Association of Christian Schools International in educational philosophy, and Paul Poirot of *The Freeman* in economics. Their works directed me to primary sources, such as the writings of John Witherspoon and William Wilberforce. Meanwhile, in my role as Headmaster of The Pilgrim Academy, I became somewhat of an expert on the Pilgrims and Puritans. The more I studied, the more it became obvious that anything good in our culture—including our free political institutions—came from Christianity and the Bible. It also became clear that much of what is wrong with America today is not because of Christian participation in politics, but the lack thereof.

The first attempts of Christians to re-enter the political arena in the late seventies and early eighties were important but lacked depth. Essentially, only the Presidential election was given any attention, when in reality the position of county committeeman or committeewoman was and is perhaps the most important. But, most Christians weren't even aware there was such a position.

Today, Christians are beginning to realize that being a good citizen and helping to shape our laws is not just an every-four-years event, but something we do every day—by calling the police when we see a crime being committed, by joining a local civic group, by rebuilding America's private institutions, by voting in primaries, by writing letters to congressmen, and by perhaps running for an office ourselves.

As Christians once again get involved in politics—"for the good of the nation," as John Newton put it to William Wilberforce, they need to know that this road has been traveled before—by men whose lives can inspire, inform, and edify. Working in England, Holland, and early America, their service in government helped shape the free world we are now in danger of losing. Hopefully, these role models can inspire us to restore moral sanity, family values, and limited government to our nation.

Chapter One

Edward VI:
Good King Edward

On the day of his birth, church bells tolled throughout England, bonfires were lit on hillsides, and people danced in the streets. "We all hungered after a prince so long," wrote the great reformer Hugh Latimer, "that there was as much rejoicing as at the birth of John the Baptist."[1]

Edward VI, Henry the VIII's only son, was born on 12 October 1537. Although he died at an early age, his Christian convictions had a profound influence on the history of England.

Known to church history as "England's Josiah," Edward VI was a dedicated Christian and sought to rule his kingdom in a Christian manner. He encouraged preachers like John Knox and Hugh Latimer, set up Christian schools, and encouraged the spread of the Reformation. When he attended services, he would stand when the Scriptures were read and take notes during the sermon. His short reign was regarded so highly that Mark Twain, when seeking a time and prince for his classic of historical fiction, *The Prince and the Pauper*, picked sixteenth-century England and young Edward Tudor. In the story, the prince becomes wise by exchanging places with a peasant, learning firsthand the trials and tribulations of the average Englishman.

But, it wasn't from a sixteenth-century pauper that Edward gained his wisdom to rule—it was from a "Pauper" who lived 1500 years before, the Lord Jesus Christ.

As the son of the infamous Henry VIII, he was an unlikely candidate to become a truly Christian king. Henry had six wives, of which only one managed to survive him. In order to divorce his first wife, he broke away from the Roman Catholic Church, which had refused to grant him a divorce. When his second wife produced no male heir, he had her beheaded. Throughout his life, he ruthlessly cast aside anything that stood in his way. The Bible interested him only when it could be used to further his own desires. And, if Henry's break with Rome opened the door for the Reformation, it was only because of "the Gospel light that dawned in Anne Boleyn's eyes," as one pundit put it.

For twenty-eight years, Henry hoped for a male heir who would rule England the same way he did. Thus, when Edward was born, even though his mother died in childbirth, she was buried with great honors— the only one of Henry's six queens to be buried at St. George's Chapel, Windsor, where Henry himself was eventually laid to rest.

The "Royal Imp," as some called him, was given an education as good as any given to European royalty. On the recommendation of Catherine Parr, Henry's sixth wife, a Cambridge humanist by the name of Richard Cox was given formal charge of Edward's studies. John Cheke, a professor of Greek in the same university, was appointed his regular tutor. By the time Edward was six years old, Cox told King Henry that the prince "undertaketh and can frame pretty Latins . . . and is now ready to enter into some proper and profitable fables of Aesop and other wholesome and godly lessons." He poured over Solomon's Proverbs, learning from them "to fear God's commandments, to beware of strange and wanton women, to be obedient to father and mother, and to be thankful to him that telleth him of his faults."[2] His royal blood didn't save his hide from punishment: when he failed to learn his lessons Dr. Cox beat him. Contrary to what Mark Twain imagined in *The Prince and the Pauper*, there was no whipping boy to take his punishment.

By the age of thirteen, he knew Latin, Greek, and French, had read Aristotle's *Ethics* in the original and was translating Cicero's *De Philosophie* into Greek. His education was rounded out by time spent at court, and training in riding, archery, and music making. These latter activities he shared with Henry Brandon, Duke of Suffolk, Lord Thomas Howard, and Barnaby Fitzpatrick, and a girl, Jane Dormer, with whom he practiced dancing.

Edward was only ten years old when his father died on 20 January 1547. Because of his tender age, the king had as an advisor the Duke of Somerset, who carried the title of Protector. The king's youth encouraged a struggle for power between those who would become his closest advisors; the Duke of Somerset was eventually outmaneuvered and sent to the Tower of London. Into his place moved the Duke of Northumberland, John Dudley. Confident that Edward shared his own Protestant political and religious convictions, Northumberland encouraged Edward to rule as his father had.

Recent research suggests that Edward was not the puppet of his Protestant mentors as some writers have suggested.[3] First, Edward was a Tudor, having all the precociousness and strength of will that his father had. Secondly, being a twelve-year-old in 1549 was completely different than it is today. In the sixteenth century—when the average English nobleman lived to be only thirty-five years old—a twelve-year-old was often regarded as a man. Twelve-year-olds fulfilled important responsibilities out in the fields, fought in wars, and

were sent to college. Edward's rigorous education insured that he was knowledgeable beyond his years.
Certainly, he knew the difference between Protestantism and Catholicism—his father had been a champion
of each at numerous points of his life. Thus, the Christian orientation of his reign was as much his doing as
it was Somerset's and Northumberland's. As John Calvin
put it, King Edward had "a maturity of moral excel-
lence beyond his years."[4]

The growth of Protestantism during Edward's reign
was remarkable. Henry himself had paved the way for
the revival by placing an English translation of the
Bible in every parish church. In Edward's reign, the
revival came into full bloom.

During Somerset's Protectorate, Thomas Cranmer,
the Archbishop of Canterbury, surfaced as a great
Protestant reformer. Primarily a scholar and not a man
of action, he had long been overshadowed by Henry
VIII's forceful personality. Now that Henry was gone
and the new king was encouraging reformers to come
out of the closet, Cranmer came into his own. First, he
encouraged continental reformers to come to England
and help promote the Gospel. The learned Italian,
Peter Martyr, a former Augustinian monk, arrived in
1547 and became professor of divinity at Oxford in
1549. Others included Martin Bucer, an Alsatian, who
became professor of divinity at Cambridge; Bucer's
friend Peter Fagins; John Laski, a Polish reformer;
Vallerandus Pollamus, from Strasbourg; and Francisco
de Enzinas, a Spaniard. Although the international team
of scholars came from widely diverse backgrounds, they
all agreed on certain fundamental truths: justification
by faith; reliance on the Scriptures; and the importance of the priesthood of the believer.[5]

Soon, John Calvin began bombarding England with
letters to encourage both the king and the English
reformers. Calvin saw in the king one of Europe's

greatest hopes. If England could become thoroughly Christian, it would become the headquarters for the expansion of the Gospel and a source of blessing for succeeding ages. In 1550, Martin Bucer wrote to Calvin:

> Redouble your prayers for the most serene King, who is making wonderful progress both in piety and learning. For you may easily perceive the danger in which he is placed, humanly speaking, when the papists are everywhere so furious, and when they see and know that the king is exerting all his power for the restoration of Christ's Kingdom.[6]

But, if Calvin was praying for Edward, Edward was praying for Calvin as well. Francis Bourgoyne, an English minister to France, wrote to Calvin:

> Our Josiah, the King of England, made most courteous inquiry of me concerning your health and ministry . . . he takes a great interest in you and in everything belonging to you.[7]

Burgoyne urged Calvin to send the boy-king "such a letter as would add spurs to a willing horse." "The King," he added, "supports and encourages pure religion and godly and learned men to the utmost of his power, and would effect much more if his age allowed him."[8]

Calvin immediately responded, dedicating his commentary on Isaiah with a preface addressed to "His Serene Highness, Edward the Sixth, King of England, a truly Christian prince."

> It may justly be regarded as no ordinary consolation [he wrote] amidst the present distresses of the Church that God has raised you up and endowed you with such excellent abilities and dispositions for defending the cause of godliness, and that you so diligently render that obedience to God in this matter which you know

that he accepts and approves. For although the affairs of the kingdom are hitherto conducted by your counsellors, and although, your Majesty's most illustrious uncle, the Duke of Somerset, and many others have religion so much at heart, that they labour diligently, as they ought to do, in establishing it; yet in your own exertions you go so far beyond them all as to make it very manifest that they receive no small excitement from the zeal which they observe in you. Not only are you celebrated for possessing a noble disposition and some seeds of virtues (which at so early an age is usually thought to be remarkable), but for a maturity of those virtues far beyond your years, which would be singularly admired, as well as praised, at a very advanced age. Your piety especially is so highly applauded that the prophet Isaiah, I am fully convinced, will have one that will regard him with as much reverence, now that he is dead, as Hezekiah did when he was alive.[9]

Calvin reminded the king that "when we repair the ruins of the Church we give our labours to the Lord, in obedience to his laws and injunctions." He continued:

Nor is it without good reason that this is taught in every part of Scripture and that it is so earnestly enforced by the prophet Isaiah. Remembering this doctrine, therefore, and relying on the assistance of God, let us not hesitate to undertake a work which is far beyond our own strength, and let no obstacle turn aside or discourage us, so as to abandon our undertaking. And here I expressly call upon you, most excellent King, or rather, God himself addresses you by the mouth of his servant Isaiah, charging you to proceed, to the utmost of your ability and power, in carrying forward the restoration of the Church, which has been so successfully begun in your kingdom.[10]

This introductory epistle concluded with this prayer: "Farewell, most illustrious King! May the Lord prosper and preserve your Majesty for a long period, aid and guide you by his Holy Spirit, and bless you in all things! Amen."[11]

Calvin dedicated two more books to Edward, each time including an epistle as part of the introduction. In the third book, a small volume of four sermons on Psalm 87, Calvin wrote:

> You well know, Sire, what danger there is to kings and princes, lest the height to which they are elevated should dazzle their eyes and amuse them here below, causing them to forget the kingdom of heaven; and I doubt not but that God has warned you of this danger that he might preserve you from it, and that you will guard against it a hundred times better then those who experience it without being aware of it. Now in the Psalm before us is set forth the grandeur and dignity of the Church, which ought in such wise to draw over to itself both great and small, that all the riches and honours of the world cannot hold them back, nor keep them from aiming at this object, namely, to be enrolled among the people of God. It is a great thing to be king, especially of such a country; yet I have no doubt but that you esteem it incomparably better to be a Christian. It is therefore an inestimable privilege that God has made you, Sire, a Christian king, to the end that you may act as his vice-regent in maintaining the kingdom of Jesus Christ in England. You see, then, that in acknowledging this especial benefit, which you have received from his infinite

goodness, you ought to be very zealous in em-
ploying all your powers to his honour and service, affording an example to your subjects to
do homage to this great King to whom your
Majesty is not ashamed to subject yourself in all
humility and reverence under the spiritual scep-
ter of His Gospel. . . . Sire, after having most
humbly commended myself to your grace, I
implore our good God to fill you with the gifts
of His Holy Spirit, to guide you in all wisdom
and virtue, and to make you flourish and prosper to the glory of His name.[12]

So close was the relationship between the continental and English reformers becoming that Cranmer,
with Edward's blessing, began planning a council of
reformed theologians. There was even talk of Calvin's
coming to England. To Cranmer he wrote:

As far as I am concerned, if I can be of any
service, I shall not shrink from crossing ten seas,
if need be, for that object. If the rendering of
a helping hand to the kingdom of England were
the only point at issue, that of itself would be a
sufficient motive to me. But now, when the
object sought after is an agreement of learned
men, gravely considered and well framed according to the standard of Scripture, by which
churches that would otherwise be far separated
from each other may be made to unite, I do not
consider it right for me to shrink from any
labours or difficulties.[13]

Calvin had reason to be optimistic about prospects
in England, for the Reformation was proceeding apace.
A new prayer book was published by Cranmer, which
formed the basis for the beautiful *Book of Common Prayer*.
Priests were called ministers, were permitted to marry,
and encouraged to preach in the English tongue. General professions, spoken by the congregations, took the

place of private confession to a priest. John Knox was made the king's chaplain and given permission to preach anywhere in England. Cartloads of Bibles were sent to Scotland. Also, King Edward founded fourteen Christian grammar schools. Best of all, the preaching of the Word was attended with remarkable success. When Hugh Latimer preached, the press of the crowds was so great that pews were broken, while at St. Paul's Cross, sometimes as many as six thousand people gathered to hear the reformers preach. Thus, as Ian Murray points out,

> The English Reformation was much more than a series of legislative Acts executed by the authorities. Political decisions certainly entered in, but the policy of burning which claimed nearly three hundred Protestants in the reign of Mary Tudor (1553–58) served to demonstrate that convictions were planted in many hearts which no force could uproot.[14]

The reformers, of course, were reaping where many heroes of the faith had sown years before. John Wycliffe had translated the Bible into English in the fourteenth century, and for two hundred years Wycliffe's followers—the Lollards—had preached the simplicity of the Gospel. So strong was Lollardry in the English countryside that Archbishop Chichele, in 1416, at the end of a long period of suppression wrote: "The Lollards are numerous as ever." Historians estimate that by the middle of the fifteenth-century, half the English population was Lollard.[15]

Unfortunately for England, Edward's health continued to decline. By 1552 he was regarded by his courtiers as a living corpse. Fearful that the throne might fall into Mary's—hence Catholicism's—hands, Edward and his advisor Northumberland arranged the succession in favor of Lady Jane Grey, the eldest daughter of Henry Grey, and granddaughter of Mary Tudor, the sister of Henry VIII. Northumberland arranged a marriage between his son Guildford Dudley and Lady Jane Grey.

On his deathbed, Edward spent his final months in prayer for England. One of his last prayers went like this:

> O Lord God, take me out of this most troublous life, and receive me into the assembly of Thy elect; yet not what I will, but Thy will be done. Lord, I commend my spirit to Thee. O Thou, my God how happy and blessed would be my condition if I were with Thee! But for the sake of Thy elect preserve my life and restore me to my former health, that I may be able to faithfully serve Thee. Ah, my Lord, be kind and gracious to Thy people, and save the kingdom of Thy inheritance! Ah, Lord God, preserve Thy elect people of England—maintain the true religion and pure worship of Thy name that I and my people may be exalted to praise and celebrate Thy holy name. Amen.[16]

Edward died at Greenwich, on 6 July 1553, only sixteen years old. Northumberland, according to plan, proclaimed Lady Jane Grey as regent, only to have the plan dashed when Mary rallied her supporters in Suffolk and claimed the throne. Northumberland was executed, as was Lady Jane Grey. Thus began one of the bloodiest periods of persecution in English history, the short but terrible reign of "Bloody Mary." On her orders, reformers such as Latimer, Cranmer, and Ridley were burned at the stake. For awhile, it seemed as if the only purpose of Edward's reign was to identify the leading reformers so that they could be eliminated by Mary.

A grander view of history reveals that Edward's reign meant much more. First, Edward's support of the Gospel strengthened the nation for the trials ahead.

The nation passed through the fires of Mary's persecutions and emerged, under Elizabeth, as the leading nation of Europe, defeating the Spanish Armada in 1588. Second, Edward's reign encouraged the development of a corps of Christian leaders. When Mary assumed the throne, many of these leaders escaped to the Continent, where they were refreshed and invigorated by the ministry of Calvin and other continental reformers. Returning to England, they gave us the Pilgrims and Puritans and the beginning of our "rights as Englishmen." Most importantly, the life of Edward VI showed us that there could be such a thing as a Christian king. Percey Bysshe Shelley, the nineteenth-century English poet, said that "power poisons every hand that it touches." But, it does not have to be that way. If a man yields his life to God and allows his exercise of power to be restrained by God's commands, then he does not have to be corrupted by power. May the Lord give us more leaders such as Edward VI.

Chapter Two

William Bradford: The First American

Historians have often referred to Ben Franklin as "the first American." Inventor, statesman, maker of phrases, Deist, father of several illegitimate children, a practical man, Franklin is supposed to represent what it is to be an American. But, there is a better candidate for the title of "the first American." Having little formal education, he wrote the first history book in America, now considered a literary and historical masterpiece. He was America's first great statesman. As an economist, he repudiated socialism and laid the foundation for free enterprise in America. He was the man who, more than anyone else, gave us Plymouth Rock, Thanksgiving, and the Mayflower Compact. What is the name of this first American? Why, William Bradford, of course.

William Bradford was born in Austerfield, Yorkshire, England, in 1590, descended from a long line of yeoman farmers. In his early life, he had more than his share of sorrow. When just sixteen months old, Bradford's father died. When his mother remarried, he was sent out to live with his grandfather. Two years later—when he was six—his grandfather died. Then, shortly thereafter, his mother passed away also. Cotton Mather said that in these early years of his childhood,

Bradford was subject to "soon and long sickness." Perhaps the hardships helped to create the forbearance, tolerance, and sensitivity that characterized his adult years.[1]

His parents and grandfather gone, Bradford was entrusted to the care of his uncles. Thinking that his weakness would hinder him from becoming a yeoman farmer, his uncles may have hired the local minister or "dame" to teach him how to read. Nevertheless, there is no record of his having received any formal education. Incredibly, the lack of early formal education did not prevent him from eventually learning several languages, including Hebrew.[2]

By the age of twelve, he was already an ardent student of the Scriptures. Although Bradford had been raised as an Anglican, someone had influenced him to walk sixteen miles across the English countryside to hear the preaching of Richard Clyfton. Clyfton, "a grave and fatherly old man," as Bradford later called him, was a Puritan—someone who believed that the Anglican Church was only half-reformed and that a true believer should do everything in his power to purify it and return it to its New Testament simplicity and power. Here, Bradford not only learned his theology, but his political economy. As Scottish historian and philosopher David Hume later put it, "The precious spark of liberty had been kindled, and was preserved, by the Puritans alone; and it was to this sect . . . that the English owe the whole freedom of their Constitution."[3]

In 1606, Bradford began attending services where Puritanism was preached much closer to home—in Scrooby, just a couple of miles away. But here, the Puritanism was even more radical—here was Separatism, the belief that the Anglican Church was so corrupt that Christians should separate from it. As Bradford moved away from Anglicanism and towards Separatism, his uncles tried to dissuade him, even to the point of threatening to disown him.

Were I like to endanger my life, or consume my estate by any ungodly courses, your counsels to me were very seasonable; but you know that I have been diligent and provident in my calling, and not only desirous to augment what I have, but also to enjoy it in your company; to part from which will be as great a cross as can befall me. Nevertheless, to keep a good conscience, and walk in such a way as God has prescribed in His Word, is the thing which I must prefer before you all, and above life itself. Wherefore, since 'tis for a good cause that I am like to suffer the disasters which you lay before me, you have no cause to be either angry with me, or sorry for me; yea, I am not only willing to part with everything that is dear to me in this world for this cause, but I am thankful that God has given me an heart to do, and will accept me so to suffer for Him.[4]

Even as a young man, Bradford was a man of rare conviction.

The leader of Bradford's new group of friends was William Brewster, the man who would become the father Bradford never had. Postmaster in a day when the job included responsibility for the royal mails, living in a large manor house, and with an exciting past, Brewster easily became a hero to young Bradford.

Born and bred to the manor, Brewster attended Cambridge University, but never finished his course. He did stay on long enough to imbibe the lofty tenets of Puritanism, which were then in vogue at Cambridge. Brewster left Cambridge and his classical studies to enter the service of Sir William Davis, Queen Elizabeth's secretary of state. Brewster soon distinguished himself for his sterling integrity. William Bradford, in his *History of Plymouth Plantation*, tells us that Davis trusted Brewster "above all others that were about him" and

"esteemed him rather a son than a servant." His was
the kind of testimony that every Christian should have.

Brewster might well have continued reveling in life
at court, dressing like a gentleman, enjoying the company of educated men and beautiful women, and eventually achieving high position. These were heady times
in English history. Living during the Golden Age of
English Literature, Brewster was a contemporary of
William Shakespeare, Christopher Marlow, and Ben
Johnson. It was an age of daring schemes and even
more daring men—adventurers like Sir Walter Raleigh,
Sir Francis Drake, and Martin Frobisher. Fresh from
their victory over the Spanish Armada in 1588, they
were carrying the English flag to the farthest corners of
the globe.

It was an exciting time to be alive, especially for
one in Brewster's position. But, when William Davis
was unjustly dismissed for his role in helping to carry
out the execution of Mary, Queen of Scots, Brewster
decided that he had had enough of the intrigues of
court. In 1607 he returned to his ancestral homeland
in Nottinghamshire, where his father was a bailiff at
the manor house in Scrooby. When his father died
three years later, William succeeded his as bailiff.

Here, Brewster began to actively champion the
Separatist cause. He brought in Puritan preachers,
supported Puritan causes, and helped to found the
secret congregation of Separatists. When a meeting
place was needed, Brewster followed the biblical laws
of hospitality and opened his home and larder for the
worshipers. Brewster considered himself a loyal subject
of the king, but like Peter he believed "we ought to
obey God rather than men" (Acts 5:29).

Busy as he was, and always looking over his shoul-
der for the agents of the king, Brewster took time to
teach Bradford as much as he could. From Brewster he
probably learned Latin, theology, letters, and the ways

of the world in politics. For Bradford, Brewster served as a one-man university. Bradford's subsequent career shows that he learned his lessons well. Bradford thought of Brewster as his father.[5]

Even as this little band of Separatists was growing in grace and knowledge, the forces of authoritarianism—both civil and religious—were closing in on them. Without the benefit of habeas corpus, some Separatists were thrown into jail by bishops who suspected their nonconformity. Spies were employed to collect evidence against them. King James said, "Either they will conform or I'll harry them out of this land." Eventually, even Brewster was summoned before the Ecclesiastical Commissioner to answer the charge of being "disobedient in matters of religion."[6]

The response of the Separatists was the same as that of so many Christians and other persecuted groups before and after: to flee injustice and seek religious freedom in a new land.

After several attempts to escape, the Pilgrims finally succeeded, arriving in Amsterdam on a Dutch ship. Soon after, they applied to the authorities in Leyden to settle there and were granted permission. Because of their excellent reputation for honesty and hard work, the Pilgrims were able to obtain loans and jobs which they needed to set themselves up in Holland. Bradford wrote:

> And first, though many of them were poor, yet there was none so poor but if they were known to be of that congregation the Dutch (either bankers or others) would trust them in any reasonable matter when they wanted money, because they found by experience how careful they were to keep their word, and saw them so painful and diligent in their custom and to employ them above others in their work, for their honesty and diligence.[7]

Bradford became a fustian worker while others became weavers, woolcombers, and merchant tailors. At first, the Pilgrims held church services in the homes of various members. But in 1611, the Pilgrims bought a large house to be used for church services and as a residence for their pastor, John Robinson. Left alone by the Dutch, Bradford and his fellow Pilgrims were finding that Christians could support a church without the aid of government. In Robinson's home, the Pilgrims continued to exercise the congregationalist form of church government which would have such a great impact on American republicanism. The New England town meeting traces its origin to the congregational church, not to ancient Greece, as many high-school history texts erroneously teach.[8]

The eleven years the Pilgrims spent in Holland saw them grow in responsibility, adaptability, and self-government. As Bradford Smith put it in his biography of William Bradford:

> The libertarian tradition at Plymouth, with its profound influence on American life, is not primarily English. It is Dutch. Simple justice demands that we acknowledge this. . . . Thus, during their Leyden years, were the Pilgrims perfecting themselves for the undreamed of work of founding a new nation. In religion, they grew milder and more tolerant. In business and craftsmanship they learned a great deal from the thrifty, ambitious and highly capable Hollanders. Too, the Dutch flair for efficient government and record keeping, the spirit of republicans and civic responsibility were to bear unsuspected fruit in a distant land.[9]

This was Bradford's graduate education in political economy.

The Pilgrims left Leyden in 1620. Bradford described their departure in a now famous passage which later gave the Pilgrims their name: "So they left that goodly and pleasant city which had been their resting place near twelve years; but they knew they were pilgrims, and looked not much on those things, but lift up their eyes to the heavens, their dearest country, and quieted their spirits."[10]

Arriving in New England just before winter, the Pilgrims found that they had been blown several hundred miles off course. Technically, they had no claim to these lands and no government. Accustomed to the feudal idea of having government imposed from the top, the Pilgrims avoided both mutiny from the sailors and a rebellion of the non-Separatists by composing a document we now call the Mayflower Compact. This document, in essence, was the first constitution written in America. After acknowledging allegiance to King James, it obligated the signers to combine themselves into a "civil body politic" that can "enact, constitute, and frame such just and equal laws, ordinances, acts, constitutions, and offices, from time to time, as shall be thought most meet and convenient for the general good of the colony, unto which we promise all due submission and obedience."[11] In one broad stroke, it established government by consent, repudiated hierarchies or special groups, and laid the foundation for republican government. It set a precedent for many more great statements of liberty that would come out of the influence of Christianity in America.

Shortly after arriving in America, Bradford faced a tragedy: the death of his wife. Bradford had been away, exploring the coast. When he returned to the Mayflower, he found that his Dorothy had been dead for five days, a drowning victim. Some have suggested that she committed suicide, but such a view is difficult to support. First, as Jacques Choron has shown in his book *Suicide*, suicide was virtually unknown in Christian societies like that of the Pilgrims.[12] Second, very few people knew how to swim, even among sailors, and, if Dorothy had fallen overboard, there would be little chance to save her. In his *Plymouth Plantation*, Bradford merely wrote: "William Bradford his wife died soon after their arrival."

Once he recovered from the initial shock, Bradford threw himself into the work of building the new colony. That first winter was fraught with dangers and suffering. Nearly half the Pilgrims died; whole families had been wiped out, and only three married couples remained unbroken. In the spring, seed was sown on the graves of those who perished to conceal the Pilgrim's heavy losses from the Indians.

The Pilgrims had little to fear from the Indians in the area they had settled. European diseases had already wiped out most of the Indians near Cape Cod. What Indians were left proved friendly to the Pilgrims. In March 1621, for example, an Indian who called himself Samoset marched into Plymouth and asked for a beer. Later, it was Samoset who introduced Squanto to the Pilgrims. As much as it were possible, Squanto and Bradford became lifelong friends. Without Squanto's services as a translator, agriculturalist, and advisor, Bradford probably would have failed in laying the cornerstone of a nation. With Squanto serving as translator, the Pilgrims under John Carver, their first governor, and Massasoit signed a peace treaty. With one exception, the treaty was kept until after Massasoit's death in 1661.

On 25 March, John Carver was re-elected governor. He would never have another opportunity to run for governor, for on 5 April, he had a stroke while working in the fields and died a few days later. With the death of Carver, Bradford's importance in Plymouth really began. He was immediately elected to succeed Carver and continued to be re-elected until his death, except for five years when he insisted on being relieved. Viewed in this respect, he was perhaps history's most successful Christian statesman.

One of Bradford's first official acts was carried out in defiance of English canon law: in a civil ceremony—not religious—he married Edward Winslow and Susanna White. This "laudable custom," as Bradford called it, was picked up in the Low Countries and is another evidence of the Pilgrim determination to keep church and state separate. Bradford and the Pilgrims also showed once again that they were willing to ignore the laws of England when they ran counter to the laws of God. Bradford had no problem turning over a previously religious function to civil government—after all, there was no conflict between the two. Both, in their own spheres, were responsible to God.

Plymouth's government in 1621 was led by a farmer turned tailor (Bradford), another tailor (Allerton), a printer, an amateur physician, and a soldier. None had any previous experience or education in statecraft. Yet, as Bradford Smith pointed out, they "successfully carried out an experiment in self-government which changed the course of world history."[13]

By the fall of 1621, the Pilgrims had gained a foothold in an inhospitable continent. Houses had been built, Indian corn was being harvested, their tables filled with wildfowl, and some Pilgrims had made a beginning in the beaver trade while "others were exercised in fishing: cod and bass and other fish, of which they took good store." With such things to be thankful for, Bradford remembered the fine Dutch custom of an annual Thanksgiving Day on 3 October, the anniversary of Leyden's deliverance from the Spanish. Bradford used his official position to declare a holiday, beginning the American tradition of Thanksgiving.

A few weeks later, a ship that was long-expected—the *Fortune*—arrived with more settlers, their old agent Robert Cushman, and a patent legalizing their pres-

ence in New England, but little in the way of supplies.
The Pilgrims were forced to share their meager provisions with the new arrivals. For its return voyage, the
Fortune was loaded with clapboard, beaver, and other
pelts, or cargo worth enough to pay off half the Pilgrims' debts to the Merchant Adventurers. Unfortunately, the ship's cargo was seized by a French privateer on the way to England.

To add to the Pilgrims' troubles, scarcely had the
Fortune departed when a Narragansett brave came into
the settlement and threw down a bundle of arrows
wrapped in a snakeskin—clearly a challenge to the Pilgrims' right to live there, according to Squanto.
Bradford promptly took the snakeskin, stuffed it with
musketballs, and sent it back with the message that "if
they had rather have war than peace, they might begin
when they would; for they had done them no wrong,
neither did they fear them, or should they find them
unprovided [unprepared]."[14] Bradford clearly believed
in "peace through strength." Perhaps his classical studies under Brewster had acquainted him with the famous Roman dictum, "He who would have peace must
prepare for war." But, whether he was familiar with the
philosophy that gave us the Pax Romana, he was a
student of human nature and the Bible. And, he knew
that aggression must be met with even greater force if
peace is to be preserved. Although no attack ever came,
Bradford took the opportunity to build a stockade
around Plymouth Colony.[15]

Not long after, Bradford helped set the precedent
for American free enterprise, which in the late nineteenth century and early twentieth century would make
her the most productive nation on earth. For the first
two years, everyone was required to bring all that he
had produced into the common storehouse, and to
each family was rationed out the supplies deemed ap-
propriate to its size. This system could have been from

a page right out of Karl Marx's Communist Manifesto: "From each according to his ability to each according to his needs." The program didn't work. Bradford described the situation this way:

> For this community [of property] was found to breed much confusion and discontent and retard much employment that would have been to their benefit and comfort. For the young men, that were most able to fit for labour and service, did repine that they should spend their time and strength to work for other men's wives and children, without any recompense. The strong, or man of parts, had no more in the division of victuals and clothes than he that was weak and not able to do a quarter the other could; this was thought injustice. The aged and graver men to be ranked and equalized in labors, and victuals, and clothes, etc., with the meaner and younger sort, thought it some indignity and disrespect unto them. And for men's wives to be commanded to do service for other men, as dressing their meat, washing their clothes, etc., they deemed it a kind of slavery, neither could many husbands well brook it.[16]

Seeing that such a system would be the ruination of the colony, Bradford decided to assign families their personal plot of land and abolish the common storehouse. Private property would be the order of the day. Only the tools of the colony were held in common, and land could not be conveyed (initially) by inheritance. Immediately, as if by magic, men and women returned to the fields. "This had very good success," wrote Bradford, "for it made all hands very industrious, so as much more corn was planted than otherwise would have been by any means the Governor or any other could use, and saved him a great deal of trouble, and for better content." When harvest came, he wrote:

Instead of famine, now God gave them plenty, and the face of things was changed, to the rejoicing of the hearts of many, for which they blessed God. And the effect of their particular planting was well seen, for all had, one way or other, pretty well to bring the year about, and some of the abler sort and more industrious had to spare, and sell to others, so as any general want or famine hath not been amongst them since this day.[17]

After serving three years as Governor—during which time he took another wife, Alice Southworth—Bradford asked his fellow Pilgrims to find another governor. "If it is any honor or benefit," he said, "it is fit others should be made partakers of it. If it is a burden, it is but equal others shall help to bear it."[18] He also suggested that they should give the next governor more assistants than he had. But, it was too early in the history of the colony for them to let him off, so he agreed to serve again for another term. He was a good choice: in 1625, he was still the only man in the world who had succeeded in making a new world colony sustain itself. Moreover, as his contemporaries described him, he was "loving unto all," "had a cheerful frame of spirit," "a person of great gravity and prudence . . . and for one of that persuasion very pliable, gentle, and condescending." He was "discreet and grave," "prudent and godly." Even the enemies of the colony, though they lampooned Miles Standish, left Bradford alone. He served as magistrate, business agent, diplomat, preacher, and day laborer along with everyone else. "That a man could be all these things," wrote Bradford Smith, "exercise all these authorities, and still be loved by those he ruled is close to a miracle. That he could be all these things and still avoid dictatorship is more remarkable still."[19] He was, already, the archetypal Christian statesman.

In 1627, the Pilgrims dissolved their ties with the Merchant Adventurers except for the debt which still hung over the colony. Bradford realized that the only way to gain the allegiance of the non-Pilgrims in the colony was to give everyone an equal stake in the assets. All heads of families and all single young men who were free were allowed to share in the division of the colony's property. The colony's trade would be retained as a monopoly, managed by the officers of the colony in order to pay off the debt. Bradford, for his services as governor without pay, was given a house.

Bradford's Plymouth was built on three contracts, or covenants—the religious covenant begun at Scrooby, the political covenant embodied in the Mayflower Compact, and the business contract with the adventurers in London, which later was changed to a business contract among the Pilgrims themselves. The religious contract found its origin in the Bible. In the New Testament, those who responded to the call to believe in Christ voluntarily joined the Church. Accordingly, the Separatist congregation at Scrooby was entered into on a voluntary basis—and one could leave just as freely. The Pilgrims rejected the Anglican view that birth as an Englishman meant that one was also an Anglican Christian. The Anglican Church forced all men together into one church, the good with the bad. It gave man no choice. But, the Pilgrims believed that "every particular soul must enter into a particular covenant with God; out of this way there is no life."

Out of the concept of the religious covenant came the concept of a political covenant. Thus, out of the republican church came the republican state. The governor and his council were chosen by the votes of all free men, without property restrictions, and the governor was always subject to examination or criticism by a popular assembly of the whole electorate. Church membership was not a qualification for voting, although most of the political leaders were leading church members. In 1636, Plymouth enacted a legal code simple enough that no lawyers were necessary. (In England, lawyers opposed codification since keeping the laws in a confused state meant more business for them.) Trial by jury was guaranteed, with at least two witnesses needed to bring a conviction. Capital punishment was decreed for treason, murder, sodomy, and rape. The laws were to be agreed to and improved upon by the free men, subject to alteration by them. Elections were to be an annual event, to keep elected officials responsible to the electorate. Women had more property rights in America than they had in England. And, taking their cue from the Dutch, the Pilgrims instituted the practice of recording sales of land.[20]

In making the three spheres of life work, Bradford was the key man. As Smith put it,

> As a leader of the colony, Bradford deserves a large part of the credit for this distinguished concept of government. It is a large concept, taking within its sweep not only the relations of man to man but of man to God. The church was a brotherhood, a family of the faithful. The state was to be an extension of this brotherhood yet distinct from it, founded on a separate compact. As long as Bradford was in control at Plymouth the separate administrations of church and state were maintained.[21]

One of the most difficult of Bradford's jobs was to oversee the colony's trade. Not only was Bradford under pressure to make a profit so that the colony could survive, but so that it could pay off its debts to the London investors. In the years 1631 to 1638, they sent 14,000 pounds of beaver and 1,156 other skins having a value far higher than their alleged debts. But, various swindles, including Isaac Allerton's padding his expense account, made it nearly impossible for the Pilgrims to pay off their debt. Eventually, after years of hard work and personal contributions from William Bradford, the debt was paid in full.[22]

When John Winthrop arrived in 1630, Bradford found a fellow Christian leader whom he could trust and look to for advice. Winthrop called Bradford "discreet and grave" while Bradford often deferred to Winthrop, the more aristocratic and well-educated of the two. Their friendship served often to smooth over problems between Plymouth and the Bay Colony.

Winthrop and the other Puritans' arrival in 1630 created a market for Plymouth cattle. As Bradford put it,

> The people of the plantation began to grow in their outward estates, by reason of the flowing of many people into the country, especially into the Bay of Massachusetts; by which means corn and cattle rose to a great price, by which many were much enriched, and commodities grew plentiful.

But, this sudden prosperity worried Bradford. He wrote:

> For now as their stock increased, there was no longer holding them together. And no man now thought he could live, except he had cattle and a great deal of ground to keep them; all striving to increase their stocks. By which means they were scattered all over the bay, quickly, and the town, in which they lived compactly till now, was left very thin, and in short time all most desolate. And if this had been all, it had been less, though too much; but the church must also be divided, and those that had lived so long together in Christian and comfortable fellowship must now part and suffer many divisions. And this, I fear, will be the ruin of New England, at least of the churches of God there,

and will provoke the Lord's displeasure against them.[23]

In 1639, Bradford came as close to impeachment as he would ever get: the members of the General Court challenged Bradford to explain why, ever since the patent for the colony was issued in his name, no more land was being granted to settlers. (Bradford and the other leaders, with their vision of a close-knit community of Christian believers, were apparently trying to keep everyone together.)

Defending his actions, Bradford explained that prior to this the settlers had been content to leave the debts to the undertakers, including himself. And, the debts had been so great that the undertakers were still struggling under the burden. Nevertheless, he told them, he would surrender to "the freemen of this corporation of New Plymouth all the privileges, immunities" and other benefits of the patent, asking only that the undertakers be allowed to make choice of two or three places for themselves and their heirs, and that up to three hundred pounds be paid to him and his partners if they had to dig into their personal estates in order to satisfy the London merchants. The offer was accepted, the critics silenced. Bradford had given up a personal empire which he might have claimed for himself and his heirs. A true Christian man, Bradford was not interested in personal gain beyond what was needed for his family; what he wanted was to preserve a way of life—the Pilgrim way.

In the end, Bradford's own success was Plymouth's undoing. Having established a secure beachhead in the New World, Plymouth paved the way for other settlers, especially the much larger Puritan migrations of the 1630s, even as its own inhabitants sallied forth in search of new lands and greater opportunities. Certainly, no one could expect the Pilgrims and their descendants to remain forever on sandy Cape Cod when a whole continent lay open before them. Yet, in his old age, Bradford was saddened to see that so many had quit the town. In 1648, discouraged by these events, Bradford stopped writing the journal that we know today as *Of Plymouth Plantation*. His remaining days were spent writing poetry, serving as "elder statesman," and presiding over a large family. He died in 1657—but what he and a few others founded remains central to the American experience. His epitaph might have been one of his own sentences from *Of Plymouth Plantation*:

> Thus out of small beginnings greater things have been produced by His hand that made all things of nothing, and gives being to all things that are; and as one small candle may light a thousand, so the light here kindled hath shone unto many, yes in some sort to our whole nation; let the glorious name of Jehovah have all the praise.

Chapter Three

John Winthrop:
Governor of Massachusetts

H.L. Menken once said that a Puritan was someone who could not rest as long as he knew that somebody, somewhere, was having fun. Such a view shows a lack of understanding of Puritanism and especially so of the leader of the Puritan migration to America, John Winthrop. For if true happiness is finding God's will and doing it, John Winthrop was indeed the happiest of men (actually, it was Menken who was joyless).

Raised on Groton Manor, John Winthrop could have lived the comfortable life of an English country gentleman—riding, hunting, collecting rents, entertaining guests. Instead, he underwent a spiritual battle and emerged as a nation-builder. Thus it was that when leading Puritans met at Cambridge in August of 1629, they picked John Winthrop as their leader. The son of English gentry, educated at Cambridge, and known as a godly man, John Winthrop would lead the Puritans in founding their "city upon a hill" in New England, and, in the process, lay the foundation for representative government in America. It was the Puritans who gave us some of our first written constitutions, regular elections, federalism, separation of church and state. More than any other single individual, it was Winthrop who made this contribution possible.

John Winthrop (apparently pronounced "Wintrop" in his day) was born in 1588, that great year when the English sea dogs and the storms of God combined to defeat the Spanish Armada. John's father, Adam, was devoted to making his Groton Manor a success. It was, for its time, a good place to grow up. There were fields of wheat, barley, peas, and hops; ponds stocked with carp; and a large barn and manor house surrounded by outbuildings. John, an only child, would someday inherit this beautiful piece of land and become its master.

By the age of seven, John was being tutored by John Chaplyn, the vicar of a nearby church, to prepare him to enter Cambridge University. Adam himself had gone there and had eventually been appointed an auditor for Trinity and St. John's College. Thus, each year, late in November or early December, Adam Winthrop mounted his horse and rode to Cambridge to audit the books. In 1602, on one of Adam's regular trips, John came along and was admitted to Cambridge.[1]

In Winthrop's day, Cambridge was the center of conflicting passions. On the one hand, the natural tendency of young men to seek out strong drink and lusty women was there in abundance. "Oh the grievous sins of Trinity College," lamented one pious student, explaining that a few boys "had a woman which went from chamber to chamber in the night time."[2] Yet, at Cambridge, there was also a growing Puritan presence, a presence that would make Cambridge into a bastion of Puritanism. No doubt it was this latter element that strongly influenced Winthrop during his two years there. We do know that, while at Cambridge, Winthrop was struck by fever and thought he was going to die. He turned to God for help, but his spiritual growth stopped when he recovered. He began to attend church faithfully, became well-read in theology, and achieved a reputation as a devout man. Yet, still, he was not at peace with God: "I upheld the outward duties, but the power and the life of them was a manner gone." Winthrop later wrote in his journal,

> The more I prayed and meditated, the worse I grew—the more dull, unbelieving, vain in heart, etc. So, I waxed exceedingly discontent and impatient, being sometimes ready to fret and storm against God, because I found not that blessing upon my prayers and other means that I did expect.[3]

But then, Winthrop began reading the works of William Perkins, whose writings showed him that despite all his outward obedience, he was nothing more than a vile sinner. Winthrop finally called upon God to save him: "O Lord, forgive me," and later recorded: "I acknowledged my unfaithfulness and pride of heart and turned again to my God, and watching my heart and ways."[4]

It was also about this time that Winthrop found another love—one which, by his own admission, would compete with his love for God throughout much of his young life. That love was his first wife, Mary.

The daughter of John Forth of Essex, Mary Winthrop would prove to be a faithful wife and fellow adventurer. They were engaged on 28 March 1605, and married within three weeks. Ten months later, Winthrop was a father.

His youth at a close, Winthrop now had many responsibilities. He was in the world—running a manor, caring for a wife and child, and working with his peers to create a better England. He was definitely in the world. But, as a Puritan, it was his duty not to allow these responsibilities to take his mind off God. Historian Edmond S. Morgan has summed up Winthrop's dilemma rather well:

> He was a countryman of simple tastes who liked

good food, good drink, and good company. He
liked his wife. He liked to stroll by the river
with a fowling piece and have a go at the birds.
He liked to smoke a pipe. He liked to tinker
with gadgets. He liked all the things that God
had given him, and he knew it was right to like
them, because they were God-given. But how
was one to keep from liking them too much?
How love the world with moderation and God
without? . . . It would have been easier to withdraw from the world, as the monks and hermits
did, to devote oneself wholly to God, but that
was not permitted. Puritans must live in the
world, not leave it.[5]

Indeed, it is one of the unique features of biblical
Christianity that, compared with other religions, one
can walk with God and yet have a family and a regular
job in the secular world. In Christianity, peace with
God is possible for anyone, not just a small class of
priests or super saints who live apart from the world
and its needs.

Winthrop tried abstinence, yet that wasn't the answer. He gave up hunting for a time, not because it was
wrong in itself, but because it stole his heart away from
God. Eventually, as he matured as a Christian, Winthrop
learned how to steer a steady course of godliness in a
world of temptation. Here is his conclusion in his own
words:

He which would have sure peace and joy in
Christianity must not aim at a condition retired
from the world and free from temptations, but
to know that the life which is most exercised
with trials and temptations is the sweetest, and
will prove the safest. For such trials as fall within
compass of our callings, it is better to arm and
withstand than to avoid and shun them.[6]

His constant prayer was:

O Lord, crucify the world unto me, that though
I cannot avoid to live among the baits and snares
of it, yet it may be so truly dead unto me and
I unto it, as I may no otherwise love, use, or
delight in any the most pleasant, profitable, etc.,
earthly comforts of this life, than I do the air
which I continuously draw in or the earth which
I ever tread upon, or the sky which I ever be-
hold.[7]

Having learned to rule himself, Winthrop was now
prepared to rule others.

As Winthrop grew in Christian character, he was
growing in legal knowledge as well. He began to study
law and soon was holding court at Groton Manor. In
1613, he was admitted to Gray's Inn in London, where
he studied law briefly on a formal basis. By 1617, he
was a justice of the peace in Suffolk County. As he
moved out from Groton Manor to a position of promi-
nence in the county, where he helped to execute the
laws of the land, he couldn't help but see the need for
good government everywhere.

An economic downturn forced Winthrop to seek
other means of support as well as create opportunities
to reform the government. In 1627, he was appointed
common attorney in His Majesty's Court of Wards and
Liveries. To fulfill these duties, Winthrop had to spend
much time in London away from his wife. Yet, it was
an important chapter in Winthrop's life: at the center
of power, he was able to meet consequential people,
watch the country being ruled, and see firsthand the
corruption at court.

Winthrop and his fellow Puritans did everything
they could to reverse England's downward trend. Their
preaching was some of the most powerful in English
history. They also worked to place godly men in government and pass laws that, as William Gladstone later

put it, encourage men to do right and discourage them
from doing evil. Winthrop, for example, tried to get
the right men elected from Suffolk County and drafted
a bill against drunkenness. Unfortunately, Puritan hopes
for legislative change were dashed when Charles II—
who was married to a Catholic princess—dissolved Parliament and made it plain he had no intentions of
calling another.

Observing this, Winthrop, still in London, wrote to
his wife:

> It is a great favor that we may enjoy so much
> comfort and peace in these so evil and declin-
> ing times and when the increasing of our sins
> gives us so great cause to look for some heavy
> scourge and judgement to be coming upon us:
> the Lord hath admonished, threatened, cor-
> rected, and astonished us, yet we grow worse
> and worse, so as His Spirit will not always strive
> with us, He must needs give way to His fury at
> last; He hath smitten all other churches in Eu-
> rope before our eyes . . . He is turning the cup
> towards us also, and because we are the last,
> our position must be, to drink the very dregs
> which remain: my dear wife, I am verily per-
> suaded, God will bring some heavy affliction
> upon the land, and that speedily.[8]

By this time, many Puritans had been thinking of
emigrating to America, as William Bradford and his
Separatists had done ten years before. Yet, Winthrop
was torn between staying to try to reform England and
leaving to set up a "New England." When he asked
Suffolk County friend Robert Ryese his opinion, Ryese
said: "The Church and commonwealth here at home
hath more need of your best abilities in these dangerous times, than any remote plantation."[9] But, the members of the newly-found Massachusetts Bay Company,
who recognized Winthrop's rising star, used every argument they could to persuade him to join. They told

him it was a lawful and honorable pursuit, that it would be a greater service to England to preserve a remnant that could expand and later extend its influence back to England, and that there was Scriptural precedent. "It was a good service to the Church of the Jews that Joseph and Mary forsook them," they said, "that their Messiah might be preserved for them against times of better service."[10]

On 29 August 1629, in a meeting of Puritans at Cambridge, Winthrop made public his decision to go to America. Also at this meeting, the leaders decided to take their charter with them, where officials in England would not tamper with what would become the basis of their government. Two months later, on 20 October, the General Court (like a modern-day board of governors) of the Massachusetts Bay Company selected him as their new governor (the company president). "So it was," he wrote his wife, "that it hath pleased the Lord to call me to a further trust in this business of the plantation than either I expected or find myself fit for."[11] Within nine months over one thousand Puritans were ready to undertake the journey—a remarkable feat in those days of poor communication and travel.

The expedition of four ships set sail in April 1630. Winthrop—who was a great lover (to all four of his wives) as well as a great statesman—and his second wife Margaret had made an agreement to think of each other every Monday and Friday between five and six o'clock and so hold communion together.

"Oh how it refresheth my heart," he wrote to her, "to think that I shall yet again see thy sweet face in the land of the living, that lovely countenance that I have so much delighted in, and beheld with so great content."[12]

On board the *Arbella*, Winthrop began fulfilling his duties as governor. It was at this time he gave his famous "City upon a Hill" message, actually entitled *A Model of Christian Charity*.[13]

Over one hundred and fifty years later, George Washington would bring his family Bible to his inauguration, open to the same passage that Winthrop quoted from at the end of his sermon. Puritan and Cavalier alike knew that America would be blessed, as Deuteronomy 28 pointed out, only to the extent that it honored God.

On 8 June 1630, Winthrop and his fellow Puritans got their first glimpse of New England. It was a clear day, with a fresh clear breeze bringing the fragrance of the New England forests out across the waves. "There came a smell off the shore like the smell of a garden," Winthrop wrote.[14]

That first year was taken up with surviving in the wilderness. A small settlement had already been set up in Massachusetts Bay with Salem as its headquarters. After a survey of the land, Winthrop and the assistants (other board members) of the company decided that Boston Bay should be the center of government. The first meeting of the Massachusetts Bay Company on American soil was held on 23 August. The charter was transferred to America, the trading company changed into the Commonwealth of Massachusetts.

During the first winter, there was much sickness and suffering. Through it all, Winthrop was a pillar of strength. Like many others, he suffered the loss of a loved one: his son, Henry, was drowned shortly after their arrival. The colony survived by drinking fresh water and eating clams, smelt, and mussels—the ultimate sacrifice for Englishmen who loved their beef, bread, and ale. In February 1633, just when Winthrop had his last batch of bread in the oven and had just given his last handful of meal away, the relief ship that he had so prudently sent for arrived.

The provisions helped the colony make it through to spring. Never again would Massachusetts Bay face such a starving time as the winter of 1630 to 1631.[15]

That spring and summer, Winthrop set up his own farm of six hundred acres in the Mystic River and occupied himself with getting the colony on a paying basis. Winthrop encouraged the settlers to begin trading for furs and fishing for fish. By the fall of 1631, when Margaret arrived, settlers sent the Winthrops gifts of "fat hogs, kids, venison, poultry, geese, partridges, etc."—a testimony to how quickly the colony had become self-sufficient.

The next two decades would see John Winthrop serve as governor for nine years and as deputy governor or assistant for ten others. Those decades would also see the Massachusetts Bay Company's board of directors—General Court—evolve into a legislative and judicial body, elected by the freemen.

The whole history of Massachusetts Bay in these early years was one in which power became more dispersed and less concentrated. In 1630, freemen who were church members in good standing were given the right to vote for a new General Court, or Board of Assistants each year. In 1632, the freemen were also given the right to elect the governor and deputy-governor. Previously, they had been selected by the assistants out of their number. In 1635, the secret ballot was adopted, something that didn't become standard procedure in the rest of America until the late nineteenth century. Grains of Indian corn for the *ayes* and beans for the *nays* were used instead of paper in many towns in these early years. In 1634, the people got another concession—an expansion of the General Court by gaining the right to elect deputies. Eventually, this became the first bicameral legislature in America, with a House of Assistants and a House of Deputies. The House of Deputies was charged with looking after the rights of the freemen so that the latter could concentrate on the business of making a living and serving God.[16]

Modern-day liberals have criticized the Puritans for their form of government, but actually they were well ahead of their time in granting to the individual the right to act freely within the Puritan's world and life view and in protecting him from an all-powerful government.

The Puritans—under the leadership of John Winthrop—did this in several ways. First, they established fixed elections to be held every year in the spring. In contrast to the parliamentary system, this mode of election put a continuous check on the government. Second, in extending the right to vote to all church members—regardless of social standing—the Puritans actually created an electorate larger by percentage than that in England.[17] "The question that needs to be answered," wrote Edmund S. Morgan, "is not why he limited suffrage, but why he extended it." (Morgan's answer was that Winthrop believed that just as there was a covenant between God and man, so there must be a second covenant between man and man, thus forming civil government.)[18] "Narrow as the franchise was," wrote S.E. Morison, "it cut through the community vertically, not horizontally."[19] Third, there was actually more separation between church and state in Massachusetts than there was in any other country in Europe at the time.[20] Ministers were not allowed to run for office, and magistrates were not supposed to meddle with church affairs. In fact, no minister ever held a political office in Massachusetts at any time in the seventeenth century. If Massachusetts was a Bible Commonwealth, it wasn't because it was a theocracy controlled by the Church; it was because individual lay Christians supported and voted for men like John Winthrop and the Christian policies they advocated. Church and state did work closely together on many issues, but it must be remembered that both institutions were seeking to survive on the edge of a vast, threatening wilderness. Finally, Winthrop led the way in doing away with both feudalism and heredity—two ideas that would prevail in the Old World until the late nineteenth century. In 1635, Lords Say, Sele, and Brook proposed, as the condition of their removal from England to America, that the Commonwealth of Massachusetts should consist of two ranks of men—gentlemen and freeholders, the former constituting a hereditary House of Lords, the latter electing a House of Commons.

Although the colony would have liked to have had such men of quality, Winthrop instructed John Cotton to reply that "although it was the custom of the country" to regard such men as gentry and the colony would be glad to elect to office any member of a "noble or generous family with a spirit and gifts fit for government," yet, "if God should not delight to furnish some of their posterity with gifts fit for magistracy it would not be proper if we should call them forth, when God hath not, to public authority."[21] The qualification for office was not blood, but Christian character. This meant that even Winthrop's sons could not hold office simply by virtue of their relationship to him. But, Winthrop agreed with the principle, and so led the way in doing away with hereditary office.

Winthrop could have tried to amass power and wealth for himself; instead, he sought to disperse power so that no one man could become a dictator. In doing so, he helped lay the foundation for America's system of checks and balances and separation of powers. As Morgan has pointed out:

> A group of men as sure of their cause as were Winthrop and his friends must have been strongly tempted to establish themselves as a permanent aristocracy. . . . They might readily have succumbed to the lust for power, since power lay unchallenged in their hands. But they

did not even keep the powers to which the charter entitled them.[22]

In yielding power, Winthrop committed himself not to democracy, but to God, from whom all power and dominion ultimately flows.

Through Winthrop's years as an elected official, he prayerfully sought to solve problems from a Christian perspective. When he lost the race for governor in 1634 to Thomas Dudley, he chalked it up to God's sovereignty and invited the new governor and assistants to the banquet which had been prepared at his house for his own victory celebration. "Magnanimity toward opponents was one of Winthrop's most attractive traits," observed S.E. Morison.[23] Over the years, Dudley accused Winthrop of acting too much on his own authority—loaning twenty-eight pounds of powder to Plymouth, allowing Watertown to erect a fish weir, and allowing a criminal sentenced to exile to stay until spring (when a winter departure would have undoubtedly resulted in the criminals' death). Winthrop defended his actions, but ultimately the rift was healed by something neither had anticipated: their children fell in love and got married. Soon, they would have the same grandchildren. Not long after, they sealed a deal in a manner that showed they were reconciled:

> The governor and deputy went to Concord to view some land for farming, and, going down the river about four miles, they made choice of a place for one thousand acres for each of them. . . . the governor yielded him the choice. So, at the place where the Deputy's land was to begin, there were two great stones, which they called the Two Brothers, in remembrance that they were brothers by their children's marriage, and did so brotherly agree, and for that a little creek near those stones was to part their lands.[24]

As late as 1930, these two boulders were still standing.

The two greatest crises of Governor Winthrop's tenure, however, were theological in nature. The first came when Roger Williams demanded that the Puritans completely separate from the Church of England as the Pilgrims in Plymouth had done. But, that was not all. Soon, Williams was renouncing everything and everybody: the king's authority to grant the Massachusetts Charter rested on "a solemn public lie"; a saved man could not pray in the company of an unsaved person, even if it were his wife and children, and that he ought not to give thanks after a meal. Eventually, he asked his church in Salem to renounce everyone—including all other Christians in Massachusetts Bay. Finally, he reached the point where he could not have communion with anyone but his wife.

In the eyes of Winthrop and other Puritans, such self-centered separation was a danger to the whole community—a community that was still a blizzard or an Indian attack away from destruction. As a result, Williams was censured by the Massachusetts Bay authorities and ordered back to England. But, before they could lay hands on him, he was gone, off for Narragansett Bay and Rhode Island in the midst of winter.[25]

Winthrop hated Williams' doctrine, yet he still showed compassion on him as a fellow Christian. In 1670, long after Winthrop died, Williams wrote:

> When I was unkindly and unchristianly, as I believe, driven from my house and land and wife and children (in the midst of a New England winter, now about thirty-five years past) at Salem, that ever-honored Governor, Mr. Winthrop, privately wrote to me to steer my course to Narragansett Bay and Indians, for many high and heavenly and public ends, encouraging me, from the freeness of the place from any English claims or patents. I took his

prudent motion as a hint and voice from God,
and waving all other thoughts and motions, I
steered my course from Salem (though in winter snow, which I feel yet) unto these parts.[26]

Thus, even though Winthrop could disagree with
someone both politically and theologically, he didn't
make it a matter of personal vendetta. His attitude
seems to have been: "I can't agree with your dangerous
views, and you cannot stay here. However, the world is
wide. So is America. If you don't like the kind of community we've sacrificed to set up here, then set up your
own colony. History—and God—will vindicate which one
of us is right."

Landing in Rhode Island, Williams opened the
doors of his colony to any and all comers—good and
bad. Having reached the farthest extremes of separation, he now came around full circle to the other extreme, that of tolerating anything. Writing in his journal, Winthrop commented: "Having a little before refused communion with all save his own wife, now he
would preach to and pray with all comers."[27] Some
historians have pointed to Roger Williams' Rhode Island as the first colony to set the precedent of separation of church and state; actually, Plymouth and Massachusetts Bay had already laid that foundation.
Throughout most of early American history, Rhode
Island—or Rogue's Island, as most of the other colonies
referred to it—exerted only a minimal influence compared to that wielded by Massachusetts. Winthrop was
vindicated after all.

But, even before the dust had settled from the
Williams' controversy, another controversy arose to
challenge the Puritans' way of life. That controversy
came in the person of Anne Hutchinson. Hutchinson
gained a following—both men and women—by having
Bible studies based on what her beloved pastor, John
Cotton, taught in the regular services. Soon, she put

her own interpretation above those of all others, inti-
mating that her ideas, which God had put into her
mind, were on the same level of importance as the
Bible itself. She also argued that a man's character was
no basis to believe he was saved—in other words, a
sanctified life is no guarantee of justification. The
Puritans believed this, but did not take it to the extreme that Hutchinson did: Hutchinson said most of
Massachusetts was living under a covenant of works.
And, of course, as a woman who taught men as well as
women, she went beyond the Apostle Paul's dictum, "I
suffer not a woman to teach, nor to usurp authority
over the man, but to be in silence" (1 Timothy 2:12).
The controversy broke while Winthrop was out of office. The governor, Sir Henry Vane, saw little danger
in her views, so he made no attempt to silence her.

Winthrop chafed at Vane's inaction and pushed
for action. Soon, all New England was divided into two
camps—those who supported Hutchinson and those
who supported the majority of ministers, who were
against Hutchinson. Seeing that this could tear their
little community apart, Winthrop, upon winning election to the governorship the following year, used his
influence to call a synod of all the ministers in Massachusetts. As Winthrop pointed out, "There was great
danger of a tumult that day and some laid hands on
others."[28] The assembly might have let Hutchinson off
with merely a censure and an admonition to stop teaching, but towards the end of the proceedings she began
to recount how God had revealed to her that she would
come to New England, be persecuted there, but that
God would protect her as he did Daniel. "And see!"
she concluded, "this scripture fulfilled this day in mine
eyes, therefore take heed what you go about to do
unto me . . . for I know that for this you will ruin you
and your posterity, and this whole state."[29]

This was too much. Winthrop and the other Puritan Fathers had risked too much, worked too hard to let this woman bring down their commonwealth. Her error is what Christian theologians call antinomianism, a term that comes from two Greek words which mean "against law," specifically, the law of the Bible. Antinomianists put the mystical revelation they claim to receive from God above the Bible. Thus, whereas the Puritans would say the Scriptures forbid murder, an antinomianist could say, in an extreme case, "Yes, but God revealed to me to kill these particular people," or, in a more common case, "God has revealed to me to be a woman pastor." The problem with this type of theology is that if any individual can receive revelation from God that supersedes the Bible, the Bible becomes a meaningless book. Refusing to give up these views, Anne Hutchinson was banished from the colony, just like Roger Williams.

Although his political and theological views may seem strict by modern-day standards, John Winthrop's views helped lay the basis for the American Republic. He favored what he called a mixed aristocracy, mixed in that faction would check faction, keeping any one single group or individual from becoming too powerful, an aristocracy of men of character elected by virtuous freemen. "If we should change from a mixed aristocratic to a mere Democratic, first we should have no warrant in scripture for it: there was no such government in Israel. . . . a Democratic is, amongst most civil nations, accounted the meanest and worse of all forms of government."[30] By democracy, Winthrop meant that form of government in which a majority— 51 percent—can impose its will on a minority with no constitutional safeguards. Democracy always leads to demagoguery—in ancient Athens, in Hitler's Germany, and today in America as the nation moves away from its original government of a constitutional republic to a democracy.

According to Winthrop, the family was the basis of

all society and government. A commonwealth, Winthrop wrote, resulted from "many families subjecting themselves to rulers and laws." Other Puritans agreed: in the Massachusetts Laws of 1672, families are characterized as "the root whence church and commonwealth cometh." Cotton Mather said that "well-ordered families naturally produce a Good Order in other Societies."[31]

For Winthrop and other Puritans, the family was more important than the individual—for it is in the family, with its history, its love, its connections, its traditions, its strength that lasts through generations, and its ability to survive the most violent attack against it—that gives the individual meaning and true freedom. Without the family, the individual stands helpless before the state. He turns either to atomistic individualism—moral anarchy—or seeks refuge in the group, statism. It is instructive to note that most modern nations, while allowing individuals to pursue hedonistic lifestyles, have begun to take away all the most important freedoms: religion, free trade, property, even life itself (abortion).

Because the family was the basis of society and all good government, Winthrop sought to place single settlers in with good families until they found a mate.

In foreign affairs, Winthrop was a realist. Like George Washington after him, he knew that even the most Christian country must deal prudently with foreign powers and not entangle itself with any. He played two rival French governors—La Tour and D'Aulnay—against one another and, when D'Aulnay won, made peace with him, sealed with the gift of a sedan chair which a visiting privateer had once given him. Winthrop also promoted good relations with the Dutch in New York, appealing to their common Protestantism. In seeking to build a Christian community in New England, Winthrop knew that it would be counterproductive to engage in vain warfare against every evil power on earth.

Winthrop was always willing to acknowledge the subordination of Massachusetts to England, as long as she made no attempt to revoke the liberties that they had been given. In the 1630s, when Charles I was trying to consolidate his authority, he attempted to recover the Massachusetts charter. To get it, Charles went to court; the court ruled in his favor, but, when the court sent for the charter, Winthrop adopted a well-known political tactic: delay. Massachusetts was saved when the Long Parliament finally met in 1640. But, even when Parliament informed Winthrop that they would be glad to protect the colony against the king, Winthrop, protected by the vast Atlantic Ocean, decided to bide his time and refuse their help. After consulting his advisers, he said: "If we should put ourselves under the protection of parliament, we must then be subject to all such laws as they should make, or at least such as they might impose upon us; in which course though they should intend our good, yet it might prove very prejudicial to us."[32] (The fact that the American colonies even in their earliest years—like Massachusetts here—never regarded the authority of Parliament formed the legal basis for the American Revolution. For when Parliament decided to tax the colonies after 1763, the colonists argued that it had always been the prerogative of their own assemblies to tax them and that it was unlawful for the British Parliament to tax them.) Winthrop's delaying tactics gave his Christian friends in England time to influence Parliament to issue an order "that we [in New England] should enjoy all our liberties, etc., according to our patent." When the English Civil War broke out, Winthrop maintained the neutrality of the Bay Colony, although he naturally leaned toward the Parliamentary forces.[33]

It was in these years of conflict in England that Winthrop faced his last major challenge, an attempt to undermine "the New England Way" by installing Presbyterianism, the right of non-church members to vote, and subordination to Parliament. The movement was led by Robert Child, a medical doctor. Putting his *Remonstrance and Humble Petition* before the Massachusetts Court, he appealed it to Parliament even before the court made its decision. If Child were successful, it might arouse Parliament to assert authority over the colony—not just in establishing Presbyterianism, but in all affairs. Winthrop jailed the protestors and tried and fined them for sedition. By the time Child and his supporters were released and reached England, Presbyterianism was in decline and New England's friends were on the rise. Winthrop had preserved Massachusetts' independence.

In order to protect their Bible Commonwealth from Indians, foreign powers, and adventurers from home, Winthrop picked up on Bradford's idea of a confederation and led Connecticut, Massachusetts, and Plymouth in founding the New England Confederation. After the first meeting in Boston, Thomas Hooker wrote "to his much Honoured friend John Wyntropp, Esquire, Governor of the plantations on the Massachusetts Bay; a glowing expression of gratitude in a matter of so great consequence; and his special prudence to settle a foundation of safety and prosperity in succeeding ages." The New England Confederation was a United States in miniature, an idea that would come full flower in 1776 and 1787.[34]

The winter of Winthrop's life came in the late 1640s. In 1647, his wife Margaret died, "a woman," he noted, "of singular virtue, prudence, and modesty, and piety and specially beloved and honored of all the country." The next year he married again, a woman named Martha Coytmore. Although he was sixty, he managed

to father another son. But, by February 1649, he was
sick in bed with the fever, from which he would never
fully recover. He died on 26 March 1649—one of the
Puritan Fathers of America.

Chapter Four

Nathaniel Ward: Author of America's First Bill of Rights

Many of the decisions made in Parliaments and Congresses come not out of the heat of debate or on the crest of popular opinion, but are the result of the work of scholars, aides, and other shapers of opinion who work behind the scenes. Such a man was Nathaniel Ward of Massachusetts Bay. Although he never held high public office, he was the author of America's first Bill of Rights—the Massachusetts Body of Liberties. Of him, the eminent historian Samuel Eliot Morison has written, "He is the outstanding figure in a phase of our history that has received much less attention than it deserves: the legal phase."[1] According to Morison, he helped give Massachusetts—and thus New England and America—"a government of laws, and not of men."

The son of a Suffolk Puritan minister, John Ward, Nathaniel was born into an atmosphere where Puritan doctrines were meat and drink. He received his B.A. in 1599 and his M.A. from Emmanuel College, Cambridge, in 1603. After studying law at Lincoln's Inn, he went on to become a full-fledged barrister in 1615 but abandoned his legal practice to enter the ministry in 1615. Thereafter, he spent some time traveling on the Continent. For awhile, he lived at Heidelberg, at the court of the Elector Palatine and his wife Princess Elizabeth, daughter of James I. At Heidelberg, he became fast friends with David Pareus, a learned Calvinist and a professor of theology at the University of Heidelberg. It was Pareus who persuaded him to enter the ministry.[2]

His first pastorate was the chaplaincy of a colony of Englishmen that comprised the Eastland Company at Elbing, Prussia. He remained in Prussia until well after the outbreak of the Thirty Years War. Here, he saw Catholic reaction to the Reformation at its strongest, which may have influenced his later strong opinions on Protestant unity and conformity.

Returning to England in 1626, he served for a time as curate at St. James, Piccadilly, and was promoted to the pastorate at Stondon Massey, Essex. As a nonconformist, he was constantly under suspicion for his Puritan views. For awhile, he was protected by a wealthy nobleman, Nathanial Rich. Archbishop William Laud, however, finally took steps to excommunicate him. In 1633, Laud recorded:

> Having heretofore often long patience and often conference proceeded against Nathaniel Ward, parson of Stondon in Essex, to excommunication and deprivation for refusing to subscribe to the articles established by the canon of the church . . . I have now left him under sentence of excommunication.[3]

Like many other Puritans, Ward decided it was time to pull up stakes and take refuge in Massachusetts—a project to which he had already contributed much. Such a decision must have been difficult for a man of fifty-five, in an age when thirty-five years was the average life-span of an English nobleman. Yet, here he was—a man of the world, a lover of good company and good conversation—settling in the most remote and isolated town in New England, the town of Ipswich (known to the Indians as Agawam).

Despite its remoteness, Ward said there were still bad influences in the town, "ill and doubtful persons . . . drinking and pilfering," and, in his opinion, the town should be more "careful on whom they bestow lots."[4] Ward said that such a town could not tolerate such bad apples for four reasons. First, there was the town's and church's basic testimony to be kept. Second, "the less of Satan's kingdom we have in our town, the more of God's patience and blessing we may expect." Third, as a frontier town on the edge of civilization they needed "a strong and homogeneous spirit and people." Finally, there were the children to think of: the parents hadn't taken them halfway across the earth to be raised with ungodly influences. Ward agreed with the basic Puritan belief that "strict discipline . . . was more needful in plantations than in a settled state."[5] The Puritans have often been criticized for their strict rules, but, without them, they very well may have been swallowed up by the wilderness, as happened to many other colonies both before and after.[6]

In 1638, Ward was asked to lead a committee charged with developing a body of laws for the new colony. The colony had been functioning fairly well without one, establishing laws as experience warranted. But, there was always the possibility that without a written code some future magistrate would usurp too much power to himself or infringe upon the rights of colonists. As John Winthrop recorded in 1635, "the deputies having conceived great danger to our state in regard that our magistrates, for want of positive laws, in many cases might proceed according to their discretions, it was agreed that some men should be appointed to frame a body of laws in resemblance to a Magna Carta, which . . . should be received for fundamental laws."[7]

The first committee had delayed—not willing to antagonize the English government by passing any laws contrary to those of England (as stipulated in the charter), while a second committee, led by John Cotton, produced a law code known as *Moses, his Judicialls*. This code was rejected—for reasons unknown—although its advocacy of life tenure for magistrates was probably repugnant to the freeman. (Annual elections were already becoming an accepted way of life in New England.)

So, it was left to Ward to develop a law code which would not offend England, would reflect Biblical morality, and be in tune with whatever laws the colony had already developed. It was hoped that he—having served as a barrister, as well as a minister—could produce a document acceptable to the majority in Massachusetts.

In 1639, Ward and his committee submitted two codes to the General Court and asked them to choose between the two. One was the *Moses, his Judicialls*, the other, Ward's. A new committee combined the two codes. Then, they were sent to the towns so that they might "ripen their thoughts on the subject." Ward didn't agree with this latter procedure, thinking it smacked too much of pure democracy. Like most of the Puritans, he believed in a natural aristocracy of talent and godliness that arose in a society that should provide aggressive leadership and help guide the common man into a free society. (As the twentieth century has shown, democracy is no guarantee of freedom. Many dictators have been elected rulers.) "I suspect both Commonwealth and Churches have descended too low already: I see the spirits of people run high, and what they get they hold," wrote Ward. "They may not be their proper and lawful liberties, but I question whether it be of God to interest the inferior sort in that which should be reserve."[8]

Nevertheless, Ward's Body of Liberties was accepted and formally adopted in November 1641.

"This session [of the General Court] continued three weeks," wrote John Winthrop in his journal, "and established 100 laws, which were called the Body of Liberties. They had been composed by Mr. Nathaniel Ward (sometime pastor of the church of Ipswich; he had been a minister in England and formerly a student and practiser in the course of the common law)."[9]

Samuel Eliot Morison has written:

> the Body of Liberties is not popular with those writers who enjoy picturing the founders of New England as a set of cruel and crack-brained religious fanatics. For the entire code shows the hand of a man familiar with the principles of English law and the securities of English liberty. Many of the provisions derived from the Mosaic law are more humane than those of contemporary common law.[10]

Because of the influences of the Bible, the Body of Liberties was perhaps the most advanced legal code of its time and presaged the United States Bill of Rights.

Ward started from the premise that all law originated with God: "Moral laws, royal prerogatives, popular liberties, are not of Man's making or giving, but God's: Man is but to measure them out by God's Rule: which of man's wisdom cannot reach, Man's experience must mend."[11]

In the preamble and its first provision, one can almost see the germ of the U.S. Constitution:

> The free fruition of such liberties Immunities and priveledges as humanitie, Civilitie, and Christianitie call for as due to every man in his place and proportion without impeachment and infringement hath ever bene and ever will be the tranquillitie and Stabilitie of Churches and

Commonwealths. And the deniall or deprivall thereof, the disturbance if not the ruine of both.

We hould it therefore our dutie and safetie whilst we are about the further establishing of this Government to collect and expresse all such freedomes as for present we foresee may concerne us, and our posteritie after us, and to ratify them with our sollemne consent.

Wee doe therefore this day religiously and unanimously decree and confirme these following Rites, liberties and priveledges concerneing our Churches, and Civill State to be respectively impartiallie and inviolably enjoyed and observed throughout our Jurisdiction for ever.

1. No mans life shall be taken away, no mans honour or good name shall be stayned, no mans person shall be arested, restrayned, banished, dismembred, nor any wayes punished, no man shall be deprived of his wife or children, no mans goods or estaite shall be taken away from him, nor any way indammaged under colour of law or Countenance of Authorities, unlesse it be by vertue or equitie of some expresse law of the Country waranting the same, established by a generall Court and sufficiently published, or in case of the defect of a law in any parteculer case by the word of God.[12]

In addition to protecting life, liberty, and property from arbitrary government, the Body of Liberties went on to prohibit feudal dues and give foreigners complete protection under the laws. It improved upon the laws of England. Servants could not receive more than forty lashes, and theft was not punishable by death, as it was in England. In England, a man could legally punish his wife with a "reasonable instrument"; the Body of Liberties, on the other hand, protected a woman from bodily correction from her husband, "unless it be in his own defense upon his assault."

Cruelty to animals was forbidden. The government could not grant monopolies. No one was allowed to defend another for pay: the legal profession was virtually outlawed. (A lawyer himself, Ward saw the dangers presented by a large class of lawyers—high-paid experts getting criminals off on a technicality, problems complicated by legal battles, and laws kept complicated and in a state of flux to keep their services in demand.)

The Body of Liberties further stipulated that taxes could not be levied on property a man held in England and that the freemen had the right to refuse to reelect magistrates without cause, contrary to what John Cotton had written in *Moses, his Judicialls*.[13] In 1648, the Body of Liberties was improved upon and served as the foundation for the rest of American law.

Ward retired from the pastorate in 1636, battling poor health. For the next ten years, he lived at Ipswich and was active in promoting the settlement of towns such as Andover and Haverhill.

Towards the end of his life, he turned from preaching and lawmaking to literature. In 1645 and 1646, he wrote a book that would give him a permanent place in American literature—*The Simple Cobbler of Aggawam*.[14] Essentially, the book is a serious but witty argument against extravagant fashions, arbitrary government, and religious toleration. We already know about Ward's fears of arbitrary government (within the context of a Christian state), but his views on toleration deserve some explanation.

"I dare aver," wrote Ward in *The Simple Cobbler*, "that God does nowhere in His Word tolerate Christian states to give toleration to such adversaries of His truth, if they have power in their hands to suppress them." To Ward, he that tolerates another religion "either doubts of his own or is not sincere in it." Ward also saw—correctly—that a country that tolerated beliefs other than Christianity "must give liberty of conscience and conversation in their moral laws."[15]

In Ward's day, there were no societies that practiced toleration—except perhaps Holland—so his views were not unusual.[16] Ward, who had lived in Germany, was perhaps thinking of the forty-plus German states, where most of the rulers had decided for either Catholicism or Protestantism. Theoretically, one could move to the country or canton of his religious choice.

Ward did not address the possibility that one's religion by its very nature could incorporate toleration. It could be argued, for example, that toleration came not out of doubt or insincerity, but out of the strong conviction that one's faith can only be advanced by peaceful means. Jesus Christ never used force to advance His teachings or morality, claiming that His kingdom was "not of this world" and that a man must be born again, not forced to assent to Christianity.

Moreover, as Roland Bainton has pointed out in *The Travail of Religious Liberty*, the Calvinistic strain in many Protestant groups caused them to have a firm belief in God's sovereignty and man's powerlessness in salvation.[17] Such views led to toleration because they believed that only the Holy Spirit could force a man to believe. Ultimately, in the West, toleration grew out of the efforts of dissenters fighting for the freedom to practice their beliefs. To a great extent, most minority rights in the Western world came about as a result of this battle. Since Bible-believing Christians have almost always been in the minority, toleration has worked to their advantage and against those who would forbid any preaching of the Gospel.

The Simple Cobbler was published in England in 1647, appearing in bookstores in England at about the same time Ward himself returned from America. In June, 1647, during the English Civil War, Ward was invited to preach before the House of Commons. Here, he was bold to defend the king and suggest that Cromwell's Army lay down its arms and leave the people and the liberty they had won. His advice was not taken, and more violence followed over the next five years. Meanwhile, Ward returned to his duties as a parish minister, preaching each Sunday at Shenfield. Nathaniel Ward died sometime in 1652, leaving behind *The Simple Cobbler*, America's first Bill of Rights, and the reputation of having an unusual sense of humor.

An unusual sense of humor? That's right, for on one occasion he said: "I have two comforts to live upon: the perfections of Christ, and the imperfections of all Christians." Over the mantle of his house in Ipswich, a former occupant is said to have carved three words representing the sum of Puritan ethics: sobriety, justice, and piety. Ward added the word laughter.[18] For Ward, being able to laugh at oneself was an essential part of being a good Puritan or, for that matter, a good Christian statesman.

Chapter Five

John Witherspoon: Son of Liberty

On 4 July 1776, the Declaration of Independence lay on the table of Independence Hall in Philadelphia. Two days earlier, Richard Henry Lee's resolution for independence had been adopted, and now the time was at hand when each delegate would put pen to paper, thus committing his life, his fortune, and his sacred honor to a future darkened by clouds of war. If their bid for liberty failed, those who signed would be the first to be hanged from a British noose.

Sensing the urgency of the moment, John Witherspoon of New Jersey rose to speak:

> There is a tide in the affairs of men, a nick of time. We perceive it now before us. To hesitate is to consent to our own slavery. That noble instrument upon your table, which ensures immortality to its author, should be subscribed this very morning by every pen in this house. He that will not respond to its accents and strain every nerve to carry into effect its provisions is unworthy the name of freeman. For my own part, of property I have some, of reputation more. That reputation is staked, that property is pledged, on the issue of this contest; and although these gray hairs must soon descend

into the sepulchre, I would infinitely rather that
they descend thither by the hand of the executioner than desert at this crisis the sacred cause
of my country.[1]

Witherspoon's words gave voice to the sentiments of
the majority of delegates, and, on 4 July, America declared her independence.

Born in Scotland in 1723, the son of Rev. and Mrs.
James Witherspoon, John was reared on stories of the
Scottish Covenanters, who in years past had stood for
both religious and political liberty. His mother taught
him to read the Bible by age four, and soon he was
quoting from memory large portions of the New Testament, as well as many of Watt's Psalms and Hymns.

At the age of five, Witherspoon entered the ancient grammar school at Haddington, four miles dis-
tance from his home in Gifford. Biblical principles
were taught right along with academics. The multipli-
cation table, for instance, was printed on the back of
the *Shorter Catechism*. In between studies and church,
he spent his time fishing, golfing (the national sport),
horseback-riding, and curling, an early form of ice
hockey. At the age of thirteen, with an excellent knowledge of Latin, Greek, and French, he was pronounced
ready to enter the University of Edinburgh.

At Edinburgh, Witherspoon fell under the spell of
Professor Drummond in Greek, Professor Stewart in
Natural Philosophy, and Dr. Stevenson in logic and
English literature. Stevenson, in particular, kindled in
Witherspoon a love of good literature, an emphasis on
good form and style, and an interest in the English
language. Later, Witherspoon's studies in language
would lead him to coin the term *Americanism*, which
referred to words and phrases peculiar to American
English. Witherspoon defended his Latin thesis, *On the
Immortality of the Soul*, on 23 February 1735, at the age
of sixteen, and was awarded the Master of Arts degree
after three more years of study.[2]

For two years after his graduation, Witherspoon worked with his father in Gifford until he received a call from a congregation in Beith. He built up a great library and studied late into the night, using three or four times as many candles as the average family in his parish. Inbetween studies, he found time to court and marry Elizabeth Montgomery of Craighouse.

At Beith, Witherspoon made his first foray into politics, only it was ecclesiastical politics. On one side were the Moderates—wealthy, well-educated people caught up in the heady philosophy of the Enlightenment, and the Popular, or Evangelical Party, composed mostly of the more conservative common people. Witherspoon sided with the Evangelicals, making his stand public through the publication of a scathing attack on the Moderates entitled *The Ecclesiastical Characteristics, or the Arcana of Church Polity* (1753). Satirizing the "Moderate Men," Witherspoon listed the characteristics of what the Moderates thought was a good preacher:

> I. All Ecclesiastical persons of whatever rank, whether principals of colleges, professors of divinity, ministers or even probationers, that are suspected of heresy, are to be esteemed men of great genius, vast learning, and uncommon worth; and are by all means to be supported and protected.
>
> II. When any man is charged with loose practices, or tendencies to immorality, he is to be screened and protected as much as possible; especially if the faults laid to his charge be, as they are incomparably well termed in a sermon preached by a hopeful youth, that made some noise lately, "good humored vices."
>
> III. It is a necessary part of the character of a moderate man to speak of the Confession of Faith but with a sneer; to give sly hints that he

does not thoroughly believe it, and to make the word of Orthodoxy a term of contempt and reproach.

IV. A good preacher must not only have all the above and subsequent principles of moderation in him, as the source of everything that is good, but must, over and above, have the following special marks and signs of a talent for preaching: 1st. His subjects must be confined to social duties. 2d. He must recommend them only from rational considerations, viz., the beauty and comely proportions of virtue and its advantages in the present life, without any regard to a future state of more extended self-interest. 3d. His authorities must be drawn from heathen writers; none, or as few as possible, from Scripture. 4th. He must be very unacceptable to the common people.

V. A minister must endeavor to acquire a great degree of politeness in his carriage and behaviour, and to catch as much of the air and manner of a fine gentleman, as possibly he can.

VI. It is not only unnecessary for a moderate man to have much learning, but he ought to be filled with a contempt of all kinds of learning but one—which is to understand Leibnitz's scheme well, the chief parts of which are so beautifully painted and so harmoniously sung by Lord Shaftesbury, and which has been so well licked into form and method by the late immortal Mr. Hutcheson.

VII. A moderate man must endeavor, as much as he handsomely can, to put off any appearances of devotion and avoid all unnecessary exercises of religious worship whether public or private.

VIII. In church settlements, which are the principal causes that come before ministers for judgement, the only thing to be regarded is, who the patron and the great and noble heritors are for; the inclinations of the common people are to be utterly despised.

IX. While a settlement is carrying on, the candidate against whom there is a strong opposition from the people must be looked upon and everywhere declared to be a man of great worth and remarkable abilities; provided always that if ever the same person, after he is settled, be at pains and succeed in gaining the people's affections, he shall then fall as much below the ordinary standard in his character as before he was raised above it.

X. Whenever we have got a settlement decided over the body, perhaps, of the whole people in the parish, by a majority in the General Assembly, the victory should be improved by appointing some of the orthodox opposers of the settlement to execute it, especially those of them that pretend a scruple of conscience at having an active hand in any such settlement.

XI. The character, which moderate men give their adversaries, of the orthodox party, must always be that of "knaves" or "fools"; and, as occasion serves, the same person (if it will pass) may be represented as a "knave" at one time and a "fool" at another.

XII. As to the world in general, a moderate man is to have great charity for Atheists and Deists in principle, and for persons that are loose and vicious in their practice, but none at all for those that have a high profession of religion and a great pretence to strictness in their walk and conversation.

XII. All moderate men are joined together in
the strictest bond of union, and do never fail to
support and defend one another to the utmost
be the cause they are engaged in what it will.[3]

The difference between the Moderates' and the
Evangelicals' views of the nature of man is illustrated
by an incident that occurred in Greyfriars Church in
Edinburgh. In a morning discourse, Dr. Robertson, a
leader of the Moderates, declared, "So beautiful is virtue, and so strong is man's natural love of it, that were
virtue personified to descend from heaven, all the world
would fall down and worship." Later that afternoon,
conservative preacher Dr. Erskine had a chance to fill
the same pulpit. "Virtue personified did indeed once
come into the world in the person of Jesus Christ,"
said Erskine, "but instead of worshipping, the world
crucified Him—so little love has the world for virtue."[4]

Witherspoon's book made him the natural leader
of the Evangelical Party. Even though his orthodox
views were losing ground in Scotland, he was growing
in fame in the more theologically conservative American colonies. Eventually, he accepted a call to the pastorate in Paisley (where the well-known design was
developed), where Witherspoon preached to over fifteen hundred each Sunday. In 1764, the University of
St. Andrews awarded him an honorary doctorate in
divinity, and he received invitations to fill influential
reformed pulpits both in Dublin and Rotterdam.

When an opening occurred for the presidency of
the College of New Jersey, Witherspoon's name immediately came up and was approved by the Trustees. It
was thought that Witherspoon, as an outsider, could
bring together the Old Light and the New Light factions in the Presbyterian Church. His warm evangelical
spirit would appeal to the New Lights, while his experience and academic credentials would be impressive
to Old Side Presbyterians.

After careful negotiations and some pleading by Princeton alumnus Benjamin Rush (who convinced Mrs. Witherspoon to make the move), Witherspoon accepted the call.[5]

Arriving in America in 1766, Witherspoon plunged into his new task with vigor. One of his first jobs was to get the college on a sound financial footing. Unlike many college administrators today who go begging at the public trough, Witherspoon could not appeal for federal aid. Princeton was totally supported by tuitions and voluntary contributions. Within two years, Witherspoon's fund-raising efforts (even George Washington contributed) brought Princeton back from the brink of bankruptcy.

After laying a sound foundation for school finances, Witherspoon turned his attention to educational reform. He was the first to use the lecture method at Princeton. Previously, instructors had assigned readings and then quizzed their students in class. He also set up a grammar school, authored several works on child-rearing, introduced modern languages into the college curriculum, and taught a course on moral philosophy.

Witherspoon's activities at Princeton were brought to an abrupt halt by the outbreak of the War for Independence. Like most Americans, Witherspoon was at first slow to embrace the cause of independence, hoping instead for a reconciliation of the two countries based on the restoration of full English rights for the colonials—in particular, the right of their own little parliaments to tax them and make their laws, under the overall jurisdiction of the king.

Witherspoon grew increasingly concerned, however, with the attempt of the British to install an Anglican bishop over the American colonies. He viewed this as the first step toward an ecclesiastical tyranny over the colonies, of which the Quebec Act was also a part (the

Quebec Act extended French law, which meant no trial
by jury, and allowed Roman Catholocism into the Ohio
Valley). Witherspoon understood that religious liberty—
man's freedom to own his conscience—was inextricably
intertwined with political and economic liberty: "There
is not a single instance in history," he wrote, "in which
civil liberty was lost, and religious liberty preserved
entire. If, therefore, we yield up our temporal property, we at the same time deliver the conscience into
bondage."

When hostilities broke out, and continued for about
a year with no end in sight, Witherspoon felt that it
was his duty to set forth the issue from the pulpit. In
what is perhaps his most celebrated sermon, *The Dominion of Providence Over the Passion of Men*, Witherspoon
said:

> The cause in which America is now in arms, is
> the cause of justice, of liberty, and of human
> nature. So far as we have hitherto proceeded, I
> am satisfied that the confederacy of the colo-
> nies has not been the effect of pride, resent-
> ment, or sedition, but of a deep and general
> conviction that our civil and religious liberties,
> and consequently in a great measure the tem-
> poral and eternal happiness of us and our pos-
> terity, depended on the issue.[6]

Witherspoon went on to say that Americans would
need "pure manners," "bravery," "economy," and "fru-
gality" if they wanted to win their independence.

> The riotous and wasteful liver whose craving
> appetites make him constantly needy, is, and
> must be subject to many masters, according to
> the saying of Solomon, "The borrower is ser-
> vant to the lender." But the frugal and moder-
> ate person, who guides his affairs with discre-
> tion, is able to assist in public councils by a free
> and unbiased judgement, to supply the wants of

his poor brethren, and sometimes, by his estate
and substance, to give important aid to a sink-
ing country.[7]

Even though Witherspoon may not have been responsible for swaying the Congress in the nick of time,
as tradition suggests, his participation in congressional
debates was frequent, sensible, and diverse. His custom was to delay speaking until others had laid out the
lines of argument. He would wait for the moment
when he could make a good transition into remarks
that he had once written out and had fixed well in his
mind. This made him appear to be a deft, extempora-
neous speaker.

Early on he opposed Ben Franklin, who wanted the
vote under Articles of Confederation to be based on
taxable population. Citing Holland as a successful example, Witherspoon argued that unless each state were
given an equal vote, some might drop out of the Confederation. He argued swift formation of a common
government, even though such a union might be fraught
with difficulties. "Shall we establish nothing good because we know it cannot be eternal?" he asked. Such
articles could be improved upon through time, he
concluded.[8]

Witherspoon's first committee appointment was to
procure wagons for public service, where he used his
influence to keep the government from seizing private
property without due compensation. Appointed to the
committee on clothing, Witherspoon eventually set up
an emigre' weaver from Paisley in Nassau Hall to produce uniforms for the Continental Army. His success
on these committees led to his appointment to the
Committee on Secret Correspondence (later the Foreign Affairs Committee), where he played his most
important role as a congressman, seeking the foreign
aid that ultimately would help America win the war. In
Congress, Witherspoon urged a strong central execu-

tive for America's new government and more authority
for the head of a diplomatic mission, rather than having each member report separately to Congress.[9]

His first contact with the enemy came in November of 1776, when he was given charge of four prisoners of war. He took these prisoners to Princeton, where
two of them wound up working on Witherspoon's farm
at Tusculum. Throughout the war years, Witherspoon
would be given a number of prisoners of war or Loyalists. In this role, he obtained better conditions for his
charges and successfully exchanged them for American
prisoners. "As governor of a body of young but chronic
objectors at college," wrote Prof. Varnum Lansing
Collins, "the president was in some subtle way equipped
for settling the very real grievances of older and more
genuine captives."[10]

Late in 1776, Witherspoon told the student body
that it would probably be impossible for the college to
continue under the circumstances of war. From an
unknown student's diary we have this account:

> Our worthy president deeply affected at this
> solemn scene entered the Hall where the stu-
> dents were collected, and in a very affecting
> manner informed us of the improbability of
> continuing there longer in peace; and after giv-
> ing us several suitable instructions and much
> good advice very affectionately bade us fare-
> well. Solemnity and distress appeared almost in
> every countenance. Several students that had
> come 5 to 600 miles and just got settled in
> College, were now obliged under every disad-
> vantage to return with their effects or leave them
> behind, which several through impossibility of
> getting a carriage at so confused a time, were
> obliged to do, and lost their all.[11]

Eventually, both British and American forces took
turns occupying Nassau Hall. Windows were broken,

woodwork ripped up, pews chopped up for firewood, and horses stabled in church. Witherspoon was obviously distraught to see this center of Christian learning devastated. In a letter to Thomas Jefferson, Thomas Nelson, Jr., wrote: "Old Weatherspoon has not escaped their fury. They have burnt his Library. It grieves him much that he has lost his controversial Tracts. He would lay aside the Cloth to take revenge on them. I believe he would send them to the Devil if he could, I am sure he would."[12]

Of British atrocities in New Jersey Witherspoon wrote: "There is scarcely a virgin to be found in the part of the country that they have passed thro' and yet all the Jersies will not turn out. Rapes, Rapine, and Murder are not sufficient to raise the Resentment of these people."[13]

Witherspoon's Christian convictions and good sense were evident in his opposition to Thomas Paine's appointment as secretary to the Committee on Foreign Affairs. Not only were Paine's atheist views unacceptable to Witherspoon, but Witherspoon claimed that when Paine and he had worked together on the *Pennsylvania Magazine*, Paine had been inconsistent and unreliable. Paine received the appointment but, true to Witherspoon's prediction, had to be dismissed for "breach of confidence."[14]

In the early years of the Continental Congress, congressmen worked without salary. Witherspoon needed his presidential salary and did his best to keep Princeton alive. In 1777, the faculty consisted of one teacher, Professor Churchill, and one tutor. Witherspoon visited whenever he could leave Philadelphia.

In May of 1777, Witherspoon was appointed to the Committee on Finance. Witherspoon became fast friends with Robert Morris, and together they worked to raise the necessary funds to carry on the war. From his position on the finance committee, Witherspoon spoke out against issuing too much paper money, against reneging on interest of government bonds, and against paying army supplies by commission rather than by contract.

A completely different subject that came up in Congress was how to elect major generals. Some congressmen suggested that major generals be elected by their officers. Witherspoon, publicly recalling the year he let the senior class elect its own honor men and the fiasco that followed, argued that only Congress should appoint major generals. This would retain civilian control of the army and reduce the possibility of military domination of the government. Congress ultimately agreed with Witherspoon.

In September of 1777, Congress was put to flight as the British marched on Philadelphia. While many of its members attempted to meet in Lancaster, Pennsylvania, Witherspoon returned to Princeton. Here, he heard tragic news from the latest battle, at Germantown. Among those killed in action was his son James. The report was that one cannonball had killed both James and General Nash. Like most of the other Founding Fathers, Witherspoon paid a high price for joining the cause of American freedom.

Appointed to the Board of War, Witherspoon refused to negotiate with what he called Lord Howe's and General Clinton's "half offers" of peace. Other duties included reorganizing the Board of Treasury, designing seals for the Treasury and Navy departments, and naming Franklin as minister plenipotentiary. The year ended with his representing New Jersey at the ratification of the Articles of Confederation.

The following year, during an investigation of Silas Deane, he once again reiterated his longstanding contention that such proceedings should not be secret and that the public should be told the truth whenever possible.[15]

Towards the end of 1779, Witherspoon resolved not to run for Congress again, planning to dedicate his time to the college, insuring that there would indeed be a college when the war was over. But, Witherspoon couldn't stay out of politics for long: by October of 1779, he was a state senator; a few months later, he was elected to Congress. In Witherspoon's day, Congress was quite unlike the Congress of today, where over 90 percent of the incumbents are re-elected. "The Congress is changing every day," he wrote a friend, "this year all the delegates were changed but one." In 1779, there was no lucrative pension plan for congressmen.

Not all of Witherspoon's proposals were successful. In January, he moved that Congress be empowered to levy and collect taxes on imports and to oversee commerce. (The states had been inconsistent in collecting and turning taxes over to Congress to finance the war.) For many Congressmen, Witherspoon's proposal smacked of giving too much power to the central government and the motion failed. At the same time, though, Witherspoon was experiencing success in dealing with the French, where his knowledge of both spoken and written French was invaluable to the American cause.

In late September, Witherspoon recommended to Congress the request of a Philadelphia printer, Robert Aitken, to publish a Bible for America's wartime needs. Witherspoon believed that more copies of the Bible were needed to help strengthen the nation in time of trial. Congress agreed, and thus approved the printing of the first complete English Bible in the United States. There was no ACLU around to challenge the action in court.

November of that year saw Witherspoon perform his last major act in Congress. He wrote the eighth proclamation since the war began for a day of Thanksgiving. Providentially, it fell on Thursday, 28 November, helping to establish precedent for America's tradition of a Thanksgiving holiday. Eighty years later, the last Thursday in November would become the national holiday of Thanksgiving.

Witherspoon ended his service in Congress in 1782. Over the years, his attendance at Congress had been the most faithful of any member. Through all those years he never hid his Christian beliefs. He once told his former student, Ashbel Green, that he "did not lay aside at any time his ministerial character" and "in sessions of Congress or its committees sat in gowns and bands."

The war left Nassau Hall in ruins, as the British particularly singled out Presbyterian institutions for destruction. Undaunted, Witherspoon set about rebuilding his beloved Princeton. He still found time to comment on the problems which confronted the new nation—particularly economic problems. An economist, or moral philosopher, of the first rank and an advocate of hard money, Witherspoon had seen firsthand the effects of the inflationary Continentals. In his *Essay on Money*, which in many ways presaged the writings of the Austrian school of economics, Witherspoon wrote

> I observe that to arm such bills with the authority of the state, and make them legal tender in all payments is an absurdity so great, that it is not easy to speak with propriety upon it. . . . It has been found, by the experience of ages, that money must have a standard of value, and if any prince or state debase the metal below the standard, it is utterly impossible to make it succeed. Why will you make a law to oblige men to take money when it is offered them? Are there any who refuse it when it is good? If it is necessary to force them, does not this system produce a most ludicrous inversion of the nature of things?[16]

Witherspoon was also mindful of the tremendous productive capacity of the free society, not only in the physical realm, but in the other fields of human action as well. In a textbook he wrote for his students, he concluded: "What then is the advantage of civil liberty? I suppose it chiefly consists in its tendency to put in motion all the human powers. Therefore it promotes industry, and in this respect happiness—produces every latent quality, and improves the human mind. Liberty is the nurse of riches, literature, and heroism."[17]

The contract, so essential to capitalism, also loomed large in Witherspoon's thought: "Contracts are absolutely necessary in social life. Every transaction almost may be considered as a contract, either more or less explicit."[18] Anticipating the work of the late nineteenth century Austrian economists, Witherspoon touched upon the discovery that value is essentially subjective, determined not by the amount of labor that goes into a product or by government decree, but by individuals freely acting in the marketplace. "Nothing has any real value unless it be of some use in human life, or perhaps we may say, unless it is supposed to be of use, and so becomes the object of human desire."[19]

Witherspoon's greatest political contribution, however, was his influence on the U.S. Constitution, through his star pupil James Madison. Madison's political views mirrored those of Witherspoon so closely that if we consider Madison the Father of the Constitution, Witherspoon might be considered its Grandfather.

Though he was born and reared in Virginia, Madison's father decided not to send his son to William and Mary, but to Princeton, where Madison could not only study in a more cosmopolitan atmosphere, but under John Witherspoon. Madison arrived at Nassau Hall in 1769, just one year after Witherspoon had taken over at the helm. Madison, who would later become known as the scholar among the Founding Fathers, was at the height of his intellectual powers. Madison had Witherspoon for several classes and listened to his preaching each Sunday. So impressed was he with Witherspoon that he returned after graduation, in 1772, to be tutored by Witherspoon in theology, ethics, and Hebrew. Years later, when it came time to write the major outlines of a plan of government for the new nation, Madison composed a document that followed the "old doctor's" political teachings. A comparison of Witherspoon's lecture notes—which Madison probably heard and discussed—with the Constitution bears this out.[20]

First, as an orthodox Calvinist, Witherspoon accepted the Bible's teaching on the nature of man. He believed with Jeremiah that "the heart is deceitful, and desperately wicked" and was in need of restraint and regeneration. "What is the history of the world," he wrote, "but the history of human guilt?" This was the starting point for his political philosophy. Man, although wicked, was still created in God's image and had dignity, especially through Jesus Christ. These beliefs about man had tremendous implications for Witherspoon's political beliefs. It meant, first of all, that government should be set up to protect man from "man's inhumanity to man" (as well as from the government itself), and secondly, that good government was to some extent possible. Despite his belief in the utter depravity of man, he was not a fatalist. He saw that God had good purpose in divinely instituting government. In a speech to the Continental Congress, Witherspoon said:

> Shall we live without government, because every constitution has its old age, and its period? Because we know that we shall die, shall we take no pains to preserve or lengthen our life? Far from it, sir: it only requires the more watchful attention, to settle government upon the best principles, and in the wisest manner, that it

may last as long as the nature of things will admit.[21]

How to set up a government that would last—and at the same time protect everyone's liberty from the evil that man can do; to keep them from using government to advance their own selfish interests—that was the problem. Witherspoon's answer was to set up the government in such a way that a balance of power would keep any one faction or individual from appropriating too much power. Thus, even though government should be limited in its structure, "it must be complex, so that the one principle may check the other."[22] "It is of consequence," Witherspoon told Madison and other students,

> to have as much virtue among the particular members of a community as possible; but it is folly to expect that a state should be upheld by integrity in all who have a share in managing it. They must be so balanced, that when everyone draws to his own interest or inclination, there may be an even-poise upon the whole.[23]

As an illustration of how this worked in reality, Witherspoon cited the British government, in which "the king had the power of making war and peace, but the parliament has the levying and distribution of money, which is a sufficient restraint."[24] The concepts of checks and balances and of separation of powers later found their way into the Constitution and became its most distinguishing feature. If the Congress takes too much authority, the president may veto its legislation; if the president over-steps his authority, his veto can be over-ridden; and if the Supreme Court goes beyond its bounds, its individual members can be impeached. These are just a few of the many checks and balances that have kept one branch or one individual from becoming too powerful. In Madison's defense of this system, which appeared in the *Federalist Papers*, one can almost hear the Scottish brogue of Madison's greatest teacher:

> But the great security against a gradual concentration of the several powers in the same department, consists in giving to those who administer each department the necessary constitutional means and personal motives to resist encroachments of the others. The provisions for defense must in this, as in all other cases, be made commensurate to the danger of attack. Ambition must be made to counteract ambition. The interest of the man must be connected with the constitutional rights of the place. It may be a reflection on human nature, that such devices should be necessary to control the abuses of government. But what is government itself, but the greatest of all reflections on human nature? If men were angels, no government would be necessary. In framing a government which is to be administered by men over men, the great difficulty lies in this: you must first enable the government to control the governed; and in the next place oblige it to control itself. A dependence on the people is, no doubt, the primary control on the government; but experience has taught mankind the necessity of auxiliary precautions.[25]

For Madison, these "auxiliary precautions" included a system of checks and balances whereby there would be an "even poise" upon each faction. Madison believed that such precautions would always be needed, since he believed in the "political depravity of man" and that the "causes of faction are . . . sown in the nature of man."

A second concept that loomed large in Witherspoon's thoughts and later found its way into

the Constitution was the idea of a social contract. For
Witherspoon, the Social Contract was a fairly simple
idea. He believed that at some time after the creation
of man, perhaps "two or three generations" human
families voluntarily formed themselves into larger units
for protection. Today, we call those units states. There
was no coercion involved; they simply banded together
out of necessity, much as the Pilgrims and Separatists
banded together through the Mayflower Compact.
"From this view of society as a voluntary compact,"
Witherspoon continued, "results this principle, that men
are originally and by nature equal, and consequently
free."[26] Witherspoon readily confessed that all such
governments were set up by God, through the out-
working of providence in history. In the Constitution,
the idea of the social contract is inherent in the Preamble. It is "We the People" that give up a certain
portion of our resources to finance this government,
"A wise and frugal government," as Jefferson later said,
"that otherwise leaves the people free for their own
pursuits." But, the government does not own the people
or their resources. Today, we have the mistaken idea
that the government owns everything, and that it is
only by the government's grace that some of those
resources are not taxed or expropriated. For
Witherspoon and the other Founding Fathers, it was
the other way around: the government started with
nothing and would be given only that which was necessary to pay for its limited functions. As Witherspoon
put it, "Liberty either cannot, or ought not to be given
up—in the social State—the end of the union should be
the protection of liberty, as far as it is a blessing."[27]
This is the true American tradition.

   A third leading principle that Witherspoon empha-
sized in his lectures, and that was later embodied in
the Constitution, was the importance of private property. Each year in his class on moral philosophy he

gave his students the following reasons for protecting private property, and for avoiding anything that smacked of socialism:

> (1) Without private property no laws would be sufficient to compel universal industry. There never was such a parity of manners and zeal for the public in the individuals of a great body, but that many would be idle and slothful and maintain themselves upon the labor of others.

> (2) There is no reason to expect in the present state of human nature that there would be a just and equal distribution to everyone according to his necessity, nor any room for distribution according to merit.

> (3) There would be no place for the exercise of some of the noblest affections of the human mind, such as charity, compassion, beneficence, etc.

> (4) Some had laid down schemes for making property common, as Sir Thomas More, in his Utopia; but in general they are chimerical and impracticable.[28]

Madison and the other Founding Fathers agreed with Witherspoon, for the protection of private property is a major theme of the Constitution. Property cannot be taken away without just compensation, and intellectual property is protected through copyrights and patents. As a noninterventionist document, the Constitution helped to create a favorable environment in which man had boundless opportunities to obtain property and in which they could enjoy the fruits of their labor.

Witherspoon was an advocate of an extremely limited government, a government that confined itself to protection, defense, the coining of money, and possessing and managing public edifices. With the civil government limited to these functions, order would be maintained by a virtuous citizenry who governed themselves through their families, their churches, their voluntary organizations, and the guidance of the Holy Spirit. As one of Witherspoon's favorite authors, Hugo Grotius, put it,

> He knows not how to rule a kingdome, that cannot manage a Province; nor can he wield a Province, that cannot order a City; nor can he order a City, that knows not how to regulate a Village; nor he a Village, that cannot guide a Family; nor can that man govern well a Family that knows not how to govern himselfe; neither can any govern himselfe unless his reason be Lord, Will and Appetite her Vassals; nor can Reason rule unless herselfe be ruled by God and (wholy) be obedient to him.[29]

Both Witherspoon and Grotius understood that there were other governments besides civil governments—family government, personal government, school government, etc.—and that when these governments were healthy, they formed a powerful bulwark against the growth of the state.

Witherspoon never confused the state with society. The state was only an agency within society, assigned to protect people's lives and property. This was the kind of government that the Constitution gave us.

Many more of Witherspoon's concepts can be found in the Constitution. His fear of democracy ("Pure democracy cannot subsist long . . . is always subject to caprice and the madness of popular rage.")[30] can be seen in the Constitution's provision for a Constitutional Republic. His emphasis on the right of every man being considered innocent until proven guilty may be found in the Constitution. His stress on religious freedom can be seen in the Constitution's provision that the national government not interfere with religion (the First Amendment). According to Witherspoon, "the magistrate ought to defend the rights of conscience, and tolerate all in their religious sentiments that are not injurious to their neighbors."[31] It should be pointed out that Witherspoon saw no problem with the magistrate's making "public provision for the worship of God." For Witherspoon, liberty did not mean a society devoid of religious influence; it meant a society in which all sects could thrive on a voluntary basis and were free to inform all institutions—including government. In Witherspoon's day, there was no such thing as the secular state, nor was there any desire on the part of America's Founding Fathers to create such a leviathan.

That Witherspoon approved of Madison's statecraft there can be little doubt. Shortly after the adjournment of the Philadelphia convention, the College of New Jersey awarded Madison an honorary doctor's degree, indicating Witherspoon's approval of Madison's work. Then, as a representative to the New Jersey state convention, Witherspoon voted in favor of the Constitution's ratification. Finally, Ashbel Green wrote that Witherspoon approved of the new Constitution "as embracing principles, and carrying into effect measures, which he had long advocated, as essential to the preservation of the liberties, and the promotion of the peace and prosperity of the country."[32] It would be misleading to say that the Constitution is what it is because of John Witherspoon. After all, out of the fifty-five signers of the Constitution, at least fifty-two professed to be orthodox Christians, and, no matter what they believed personally, they could not escape the influence of Christianity, and they publicly acknowledged and respected the major themes of the Bible—particularly those that could be applied to civil government.[33] It was Washington, the chairman of the Constitutional Convention, who declared:

Of all the dispositions and habits which lead to political prosperity, religion and morality are indispensable supports. In vain would that man claim the tribute of patriotism who should labor to subvert these great pillars of human happiness—these firmest props of the duties of men and citizens. The mere politician, equally with the pious man, ought to respect and cherish them.[34]

Jefferson, too, was a moderate Unitarian who accepted the Bible's teachings on morality: it was the Bible that Jefferson edited, not the Koran. Even Ben Franklin, a Deist, acknowledged the Christian view of man when he remarked, "If men are so wicked as we now see them with religion, what would they be without it?" All the framers of the Constitution, no matter what their beliefs, lived within a culture that was informed by Christian values. "To them all," wrote historian Ralph Ketcham, "the Ten Commandments, the Sermon on the Mount, and the twelfth chapter of Paul's Epistle to the Romans were canonical."[35]

Madison may have come to the same conclusions about man and society without even having studied under Witherspoon. Madison's whole education was essentially a Christian education.

Madison and the other Founding Fathers could very well have developed the same exact Constitution, right down to the last jot and tittle. But, the fact remains that Witherspoon did teach Madison, and, in the history of ideas, there is a direct line from Witherspoon's Calvinist heritage down through Madison to the United States Constitution. In summing up Witherspoon's influence on Madison, James Smylie has written:

Without preaching a sermon and yet relying upon his theological orientation, Madison translated the views of Witherspoon on the nature of

man into a political instrument. While he was
touched by many influences, his relationship with
Witherspoon during his formative years was
crucial. . . .

It may also be said that the Calvinism of the
College of New Jersey was woven into the fabric
of the American Constitution and continues to
inform America's political experiment.[36]

When one considers Witherspoon's influence on
the Constitution through Madison, it is not difficult to
understand why German historian Leopold von Ranke
would say that "John Calvin was the virtual founder of
America." Richard Hofstadter of Columbia University
was even more specific: "The men who drew up the
constitution in Philadelphia during the summer of 1787
had a vivid Calvinistic sense of human evil and damna-
tion and believed with Hobbes that men are selfish and
contentious."[37] As Hofstadter pointed out, they were
realists. The result was a Constitution that assumes the
depravity of man and makes it difficult for one man,
one branch, or the whole government to become sovereign.

Charles Haddon Spurgeon, the great British
preacher, once remarked that "it is harder to learn to
say 'no' than to learn Latin." The framers of the Constitution said "no" again and again to the concentration of power. Thus, the Constitution contains many
more prohibitions than grants of power. The product
of a Christian culture, the Constitution was intended
to function within a Christian society. Witherspoon
recognized this as well as any of the other Founding
Fathers. "A good constitution," he had said just before
the War, "may hold the rotten materials together for a
time; but beyond a certain pitch, even the best constitution will prove ineffectual, and slavery must ensue."
Witherspoon knew that no Constitution could pro-

vide fundamental values. The Constitution, as Harold O.J. Brown has pointed out, "is an instrument whereby fundamental values may be protected, defining the procedures, principles, and methods whereby government can function to allow people to give content to their lives."[38] The Founding Fathers, especially Witherspoon, saw that content as coming from the Bible. When the Bible's influence on society began to wane, what was needed was a spiritual revival. "We have no right to ask for material prosperity," he often said, "without a revival of religion."

Witherspoon died at the age of seventy-one and was buried in the President's Lot at Princeton. Yet, his Christian influence on civic life continued to make itself felt for many years to come. In addition to Madison, his students included the young Aaron Burr, Henry and Charles Lee of Virginia, and the poets Philip Freneau and Hugh Brackenridge. Ten of his former students became cabinet officers, six were members of the Continental Congress, thirty-nine became congressmen, and twenty-one sat in the Senate. His graduates included twelve governors, and, when the General Assembly of the Presbyterian Church in America met in 1789, 52 of the 188 delegates had studied under Witherspoon.[39]

Witherspoon's clarion call to revival is with us today. Two hundred years after his death, America still has no right to expect national prosperity without a revival of religion. More than ever, as we approach the twenty-first century, we need men like John Witherspoon to help bring such a revival to pass.

Chapter Six

Richard Bassett: Governor of Delaware

Delaware may be a small state—three counties at low tide, two at high, as the old saying goes—yet it is one rich in history. The site of Sweden's only colony in the New World, Delaware eventually gained the honor of becoming "the First State" when it approved the Constitution on 7 December 1787. During the War for Independence, Delaware provided the backdrop for a ride almost as historic as Paul Revere's: on 2 July 1776, Caesar Rodney raced eighty miles from Dover to Philadelphia to break a tie vote and enable Delaware to approve the Declaration of Independence.

Today, the largest chemical company in the world— E.I. du Pont de Nemours—is based in Delaware, as are over half the top five hundred U.S. companies, who take advantage of Delaware's liberal incorporation laws.

Delaware also looms large in church history, for it was there that John Wesley's Methodism first took root in America. So closely have early Delaware and Methodism been associated that Delaware is generally known as the cradle of Methodism in America. It was out of this cradle that came one of America's greatest Christian statesmen, Richard Bassett of Bohemia Manor. A man who moved easily in both the secular and religious worlds—because he knew God was the Master of both—he would serve as a calvary officer, lay preacher, senator, governor, federal judge, and philanthropist.

In 1745, the year Bassett was born, Delaware was in many ways a microcosm of America itself. The northern part of the colony was urban, while the south was agricultural. As was true with most of America, there was a strong Christian heritage. Swedish Lutheran missionaries had translated the Bible into the Lenni Lenape Indian's language, and English settlers had founded towns with biblical names like Rehoboth. Many laws were based on the Bible. And, like the rest of America, Delaware benefited from a long period of salutary, or beneficial neglect, not only from England, but from her governor in Pennsylvania as well.

Delaware, or the Three Lower Counties, had been given to William Penn by the Duke of York in 1682 to give the Quaker leader's colony access to the sea. Originally, both the Pennsylvania and Delaware regions of Penn's lands had the same number of delegates in the Pennsylvania legislature. But, as Philadelphia and the Upper Counties continued to grow, Delawareans feared they would soon have a minority voice in the government. In order to reduce friction, Penn gave them a separate legislature in 1704, but answering to the same governor. Delaware, then, had the same kind of relationship with its governor as the colonies had with the king of England. As far as Delaware's relations with the Crown were concerned, the acts of the local assembly were not even sent to England for approval.[1]

Richard Bassett was born on 2 April 1745, to Michael and Judith Bassett in Cecil County, Maryland, not far from Delaware, which would become his adopted state. But, Bassett's tavern-keeper father deserted the young mother and child, leaving them to fend for themselves. Providentially, a strong man intervened—Peter Lawson, a kinsman—from whom Bassett would eventually inherit the six thousand-acre estate of Bohemia Manor on the Delaware line.[2]

Lawson taught Bassett how to ride and shoot and how to run a plantation. Then, he had Bassett read law, first at home, then in Philadelphia, which was then fast becoming the most important city in the colonies. In 1770, Bassett received a license to practice law in Dover, Delaware, where he bought a townhouse. Soon, the young lawyer took a wife, Miss Ann Ennals of Dorchester County, Maryland. Unfortunately, Mrs. Bassett did not live many years, and shortly after her death Bassett married a Miss Bruff of Talbot County, Maryland. From this union came but one daughter who later married the prominent Delaware statesman James Bayard.[3]

When the American Revolution came, Delaware entered on the Patriot side only after careful deliberation. Delaware's actions provide evidence that it was more a war for independence than a revolution, "a revolution prevented," as Russell Kirk has put it, fought with reluctance and restrained by the benign influence of Christianity. Accordingly, Delaware's delegates to the Second Continental Congress were instructed in March 1775, to avoid "everything disrespectful or offensive to our most gracious sovereign" and to look forward to the reestablishment of relations between Great Britain and the colonies on a constitutional basis.[4] When America finally declared her independence— after over a year of fighting—the Delaware assembly suspended the government under the Crown but directed all officers "to continue in their duties in the name of the three counties."[5] There were no coup d'etats, no purges, no wholesale slaughters as in the French and Russian Revolutions. Only one major battle was fought in Delaware during the revolution, at Coochs Bridge. Ten years after the war, an easygoing Assembly restored full political privileges to refugee Loyalists who had drifted back into the state.[6]

Despite its mildness compared to other wars, the American Revolution was a war nonetheless, where men were killed or maimed; wives lost husbands, and children became orphans. Bassett, then, was certainly taking serious risks when in 1776 he volunteered to serve as the captain of a group of Delaware calvary militia, one of the "sons of the Blue Hen."

He also served as a member of the Delaware Council of Safety. Richard Bassett was a Patriot, not unlike George Washington, Alexander Hamilton, and every other Yankee Doodle Dandy who stuck a feather in his cap and shouldered a musket to fight for freedom.

But, it was in 1778 that Bassett took an even greater risk by agreeing to have dinner with Methodist preacher Francis Asbury, who had been labeled by many as a traitor.[7] Ever since 1775, when John Wesley had published his Calm Address to the American Colonies, which contained a strong Loyalist argument, most of the Methodist ministers were suspect in Patriot eyes. Wesley was no partisan; he simply wanted peace to promote the Gospel and godly Christian living. Asbury, the leading Methodist preacher, sought refuge in Delaware because it was the only state that didn't require ministers to take a loyalty oath. Hiding for awhile in one of Delaware's swamps, Asbury wrote: "Satan has made several violent pushes at my soul, but he has not been able even to break my peace." A few days later he admitted:

> I was under some heaviness of mind. But it was no wonder: three thousand miles from home— my friends have left me—I am considered by some as an enemy of the country—every day liable to be seized by violence, and abused. However, all this is but a trifle to suffer for Christ and the salvation of souls. Lord, stand by me.[8]

Asbury's fears were no illusion. After 1776, anyone who associated with the Methodists could be labeled as a traitor. Caesar Rodney, the signer of the Declaration of Independence already mentioned, was convinced that the Methodist ministers were raising a force of Tories on the Maryland line in 1777. As late as 1798, Methodists were accepted into the Federalist party only over many objections. In that year political activist Barkley Townsend, of Laurel, threatened to split the Sussex County Federalists by starting an anti-Methodist ticket, declaring that the Methodist preachers were "black dragons."[9] And, even when he had attained the high office of governor of Delaware, Bassett admitted that some people still shunned him because he was a Methodist.[10] It is not known what Bassett's religious opinions were before 1778. Perhaps he was a lapsed Anglican in need of personal revival. In any case, Bassett showed great integrity even before his conversion by his willingness even to meet with the Methodists.

Bassett first met Asbury while on his way to Maryland on legal business. Passing the night at Judge Thomas White's house, he noticed several men, dressed in black, in one of White's back rooms. Inquiring of Mrs. White who they were, he was told, "Oh, they are some of the best men in the world; they are Methodist preachers." Bassett was at first taken aback: "Then I cannot stay here tonight," he replied. But Mrs. White allayed Bassett's fears and encouraged him to get to know the Methodists. "You must stay, they will not hurt you," she said.

That night, at dinner, Bassett and Asbury immediately took a liking to one another. Bassett came to the conclusion that what he had heard about the Methodists was quite false and that "Methodist preachers were not so ignorant or unsociable as to make them outcasts from civil society."

When Bassett bade the Methodists farewell the next

day, he invited Asbury to visit him in Dover if he were ever in central Delaware. Then, one day in 1779, Bassett looked out of the window of his comfortable house in Dover and saw Francis Asbury heading straight for his door. Not wanting to be left alone with this great physician of the soul, Bassett invited Dr. McGaw, Gov. Rodney, and some other friends to tea. Like Bassett, the others were surprised and impressed with Asbury's wit and understanding. According to the Pennsylvania Governor Richard Pattison, this meeting "was the beginning of a friendship" between Asbury and Bassett "which lasted for 36 years."[11]

Not long after, Judge White visited Dover on business and stayed the night at Bassett's house. Knowing of White's espousal of the Methodist cause, some of the townspeople marched on Bassett's house with the intention of punishing a Tory. But, when the mob asked Bassett to turn the traitor over to them, Bassett told them that White "was no more a Tory than any of them" and that to get to White they would have to "walk over my dead body." With pistols in his hands and a ready sword at his side, this "strongly-built," well-respected calvary captain was able to convince the crowd to go back to their homes.[12] Bassett's ultimate conversion must have come around February 1780, when Asbury was moved to write in his journal: "Went home with Lawyer Bassett, a very conversant and affectionate man, who from his own acknowledgment appears to be sick of sin."[13]

"Sick of sin." Throughout the history of Christianity, that seems to be the main sentiment that separates the true Christian from the one who displays mere outward conformity. Bassett's subsequent life—and the fruits of that life—indicate that he was indeed sick of sin, and thus put his trust in the saving grace of Jesus Christ, seeking cleansing from his sins.

Along with other Methodist converts, including

prominent Delawareans, Bassett went on to mold the
very character of the State of Delaware for the next
century. As Carol Hoffecker, professor of history at
the University of Delaware put it: "Coinciding with
America's political revolution, Methodism was a spiritual revolution that set the tone for religion in Delaware for a century and beyond. . . . Methodism thus
intermingled with geographic remoteness to produce
the peculiar character of Delaware's down-stater, indi-
vidualistic but fiercely conservative."[14]

In 1784, Bassett backed up his convictions with his
fortune when he helped to finance the building of
Wesley's Chapel in Dover, a Methodist church. Asbury
thought that Bassett would become a preacher and fill
a pulpit such as the one at Wesley's Chapel. As a matter
of fact, Bassett did preach often as a layman at St.
George's Church in Philadelphia, as well as in others.
In one of his sermons, he says to the skeptic who
believes only in what he can test with his senses, "How
could a man believe, by this rule, that he had a back,
as he could not see it, unless he had a neck like a crane
or goose?" It was simple language, but well-suited to
his hearers. Bassett could talk as easily with an illiterate
farmer as with some of the European-educated men at
the Constitutional Convention.[15]

Despite his abilities as a preacher and Asbury's
hopes, Bassett would serve the Lord in politics, not in
the Gospel ministry. But, in doing so, Bassett gained
opportunities to serve God in ways not usually open to
ministers.

In 1779, Bassett had served on a committee of
Delaware's Legislative Council along with George Rad
and John Clowes. Reporting on the Articles of Confederation that were being drawn up by the Continental
Congress, they recommended the following resolutions:
1) that the boundaries of the states claiming to own
land to or beyond the Mississippi be limited; 2) that

Delaware receive a share of Western lands ungranted at the beginning of the Revolution; and that 3) controversies regarding private land rights in Delaware be settled in Delaware courts. The General Assembly believed that the Articles were "disadvantages to Delaware" but, in an act of magnanimity, decided to join because "the interest of particular states ought to be postponed to the general good of the union."[16] Little Delaware, led by far-seeing men like Bassett, had taken a giant step towards fostering the spirit needed to create a United States of America.

After the Battle of Yorktown effectively ended the fighting of the Revolutionary War, Bassett served as a delegate in the Delaware State House. One of his first responsibilities was to help the postwar economy get established on a sound financial footing. As a Christian statesman, Bassett set about his duty of insuring that contracts were fulfilled, that the currency was not debased, and that the state couldn't become so powerful as to jeopardize the integrity of private institutions such as the family and businesses. One of the first challenges came in 1785, when the legislature proposed an act to redeem state bills of credit left over from the revolution at a rate of seventy-five to one. In other words, the dollars issued during the revolution, some of which were bought by ardent Patriots or paid to soldiers, were worth only one-seventy-fifth of their face value. This default was excused on the basis that many of the land mortgages securing the bills had been settled in nearly worthless Continental currency, thus keeping the Delaware emissions in circulation even though their security had been weakened. But, Bassett, along with his friend George Read, objected vehemently to the act, pointing out that the General Assembly had failed to ascertain the value of the mortgages still outstanding. All the money available from these mortgages, they argued, should in good faith be applied to the

redemption of bills of credit. Some depreciation undoubtedly would be necessary, said Bassett, but not as
much as seventy-five to one. To Bassett's mind, the
state would be unfairly profiting at the expense of
those who held its paper. A contract was a contract,
argued Bassett. Such a view is not only consistently
Christian, it is also good for business. The measure was
defeated, and Delaware went on to establish its economy
on a sound basis.[17] According to historian Allan Nevins,
Delaware finances—along with Connecticut—were the
best of any state after the war.[18]

In 1786, in a tribute to Bassett's statesmanship and
character, his associates sent him as one of their representatives to the Annapolis Convention. The following year, the same body dispatched him as part of the
Delaware delegation to the convention in Philadelphia.
In Philadelphia, Bassett "attended diligently, but made
no speeches, served on no committees, and cast no
critical votes."[19] Generally, he followed closely the leadership of John Dickinson. His silence, like that of chairman George Washington, indicates that he was in agreement with the general progress and results of the convention, for, as we have seen, Bassett was not afraid to
stand up for what he believed. One thing he did go on
record against was giving Congress a veto over state
legislation.[20] Thus, even though he eventually emerged
as a Federalist, he was not so much in favor of a strong
national government that he would destroy the separation of powers that would make American liberty possible.

After the Constitutional Convention, Bassett returned to Delaware where he began a campaign to take
some of the ideas used to justify the War for Independence to their logical conclusion: the emancipation of
Delaware's slaves. In 1787, declaring that slavery was
"totally repugnant to the spirit of the American Revolution,"[21] Bassett introduced a bill in the General As-

sembly "to prevent the exportation of slaves." The preamble declared that the slave export was "contrary to
the principles of humanity and justice and derogatory
to the honour of this state." Healthy slaves over eighteen and under thirty-five were to be freed without
security. Manumitted slaves and their descendants would
be permitted to hold property and to "obtain redress
in law and equity for any injury" but might not vote,
hold office, give evidence against a white man, or "enjoy any other rights of a freeman," except those mentioned. It wasn't everything Bassett wanted but it was
a start. Supported by Quakers and Methodists, the law
passed.[22]

In 1789, this Bassett signed a petition founding the
*Delaware Society for the Promoting of the Abolition of Sla-
very and for the Relief and Protection of Free Negroes and
Mulattoes Unlawfully Held in Bondage or Otherwise Op-
pressed.* At some point, Bassett freed all his slaves, but
realizing their need to gradually learn how to live as
free men, he employed them as hired labor.[23] So
strongly was Bassett against slavery that he urged his
fellow plantation holders to follow his lead in freeing
and then hiring their slaves. When Thomas Rodney
spoke against the immediate emancipation of Delaware's
slaves, everyone agreed with him except Bedford,
Brown, and Bassett. Perturbed at the dogged opposition of such distinguished men, Rodney later wrote in
disgust: "Their conduct was vile."[24] It is difficult to
believe that Richard Bassett, who was known for his
Christian magnanimity and graciousness, could have
displayed conduct that could be considered vile by
anyone. Yet, Bassett was vehemently opposed to slavery. Not only was he opposed to it on libertarian
grounds, he was also opposed to it on religious grounds.
One Delaware anti-slavery petition at the time declared
that "slavery tends to destroy that free agency necessary to render a man accountable for his actions to a

Supreme Being."[25] Finally, Bassett was opposed to slavery because it destroyed the family, the very basis of society as God instituted it in Genesis. Advertisements inviting the break-up of a slave family, such as this one which appeared in a Delaware newspaper, must have wrenched Bassett's heart: "A Negro wench and two children, one a girl of 2 years old, the other a boy of 6 years old. They will be sold separate or together as may best suit the purchaser."[26]

Bassett's attempt to abolish slavery in Delaware, which closely paralleled Wilberforce's larger scale effort to destroy it in the British Empire, wasn't the only legislative initiative that came about after the revolution. In 1794 and 1795, petitions were received by the legislature asking that the fine for violation of the Lord's Day be increased, since stage-drivers, "carriers, peddlers, wagginers, Carters, Butchers, and Drovers" were working on that day "for Emolument and Gain." Soon, a law was passed, raising the fine from four to eight dollars for working, gaming, dancing, fowling, hunting, fishing, cock-fighting, or horse-racing on the Sabbath. Fairs, considered to be breeding grounds for vice, were forbidden in 1785. The promotion of "horse-racing, foot-racing, cock-fighting, shooting matches, etc.," was outlawed because they were "frequently made with intent to vend and sell strong liquors, to the great prejudice of religion, virtue, and industry." Laws were strengthened to prevent family break-up. In fact, the only way to obtain a divorce was to appeal to the legislature. Between 1781 and 1800, the legislature granted only one divorce.[27]

These laws, coming on the heels of the Methodist revival, seem to be a natural outgrowth of changing public opinion rather than the attempt of a small group to impose their "blue laws" on others. Today, it is often thought that if prayer and Christian values were restored in public places, such as our nation's schools, our national moral problems would be solved. But, history shows that it is best when Christian morality and standards flow from willing hearts.

Despite Bassett's opposition to slavery, he was not a radical abolitionist or egalitarian. As M.E. Bradford has pointed out, Bassett "should be remembered as one of the pillars of the old order in Delaware, an aristocratic order which preserved its authority through the Revolution and into the early years under the new Constitution."[28]

After the Constitution was approved, Bassett and George Reed were chosen as Delaware's first two senators. When in the U.S. Senate, Bassett voted usually with the Federalists, yet he opposed Alexander Hamilton's centralizing tendencies. He might be best described as a mild Southern Federalist, whose Christian views came before and shaped his political views. Hence, he could not always vote the party line. He cast the first vote to locate the nation's capital at Washington, D.C.[29] In 1793, Bassett resigned his position as senator to serve as Chief Justice of Common Pleas in Delaware. It was also at this time that he helped to found the Bank of Delaware. In 1798, he resigned as chief justice to run as a Federalist for governor of Delaware. In his favor were a constituency that favored his Christian views, one of the strongest Federalist state parties in the nation, and difficulties with France's revolutionary government that vindicated the Federalists' anti-French Revolution attitude. Bassett thus carried all three counties.[30] And, unlike some of his contemporaries, he refused to serve liquor at his political gatherings.

Bassett would only serve as governor for two years, but during that time he managed to begin work on a canal to help stimulate Delaware's commerce as well as give important support to Adams' presidency. He also used his position to work for more humane treatment of prisoners. Taking his cue from the success of methods employed by Quakers in Philadelphia, Bassett recommended doing away with branding, mutilation, and whipping. Although the Delaware Assembly agreed in principle, few laws were changed. Bassett's pioneering work, however, laid the basis for future reform.[31]

In 1801, Bassett responded to a call from John Adams to serve as a federal judge. Confirmed in the appointment, Bassett resigned his governorship only to learn a few days later that the Democratic-Republicans had abolished his seat on the U.S. Circuit Court—he was one of the not-so-notorious "midnight judges."

Seeing the hand of God in what others may have seen as backroom politics, Bassett decided to spend the rest of his life and fortune advancing the Gospel.

From 1800 to 1815, his home at Bohemia Manor was virtually the headquarters of the Delaware Methodists. When camp meetings were instituted, Bassett opened up his estate to be used in the revival services and made it a point to pitch his tent near former slaves, whose Negro spirituals he loved. According to Bassett, the spirituals, America's only original contribution to the world of music, were his "harp."[32]

Meanwhile, Bassett's Delaware Federalist Party, which he had helped to found, continued to remain strong even while the Federalist Party nationally was going out of existence. In the first two decades of the nineteenth century, every Delaware senator sent to Washington was Federalist, and most of the representatives and all but two governors were Federalists. Yet, by 1815, Delaware and Connecticut were the only two states left with any sizeable Federalist Party.

Along with the other Federalists, Bassett had helped to lay the foundation of a great nation. As John C. Miller put it in *The Federalist Era*:

This dispirited little band of gentlemen had

wrought better than they knew. They had made
a parchment into a workable instrument of government; they had proved themselves to be con-
scientious, honest, and efficient administrators;
they had proved that republicanism was com-
patible with stability; they had established procedures that even their enemies adopted; and
they had demonstrated that the powers of the
Federal government could be made to promote
the general welfare. Nor did the heritage of
Federalism wholly disappear: devotion to the
Union, respect for property rights, and the attitude of mind that distrusts those who promise
too much too soon became integral parts of the
American philosophy.[33]

He should have added that they also included men like
Richard Bassett, whose Christian testimony helped to
lay a proper moral foundation for America.

In 1815, Bassett was reduced to a state of near
paralysis, the result of a stroke. Asbury wrote of him:
"My long lived friend, Judge Bassett, some past a para-
lytic, is lately stricken on the other side and suffers
much in his helpless state."[34] He died later that year,
going to a place where there would be no more war,
no more slavery, no more politics. Yet, while here on
earth, he had served faithfully in the call to public
service God had given him. As Governor Pattison later
wrote of him: "He lived to see the institutions of his
country and church firmly established. He adorned
every position he held. His virtues will live in the rec-
ollection of all who are brought within the knowledge
of his service and character."[35]

Chapter Seven

William Wilberforce: The Man Who Freed the Slaves

On Friday, 26 July 1832, one of England's greatest statesmen lay on his deathbed, waiting for the news. Would the Parliament he helped to mold abolish slavery in the British Empire once and for all? Late that day, messengers brought the news that, yes, slavery had indeed been abolished, setting over eight hundred thousand slaves free.

"Thank God," he said, "that I have lived to witness a day in which England is willing to give twenty millions sterling for the abolition of slavery." Three days later he died, ending one of the greatest epics in all political history, the story of a truly Christian statesman, "the man who freed the slaves," William Wilberforce.

The story of William Wilberforce begins on 24 August 1759, when a son was born to Robert and Elizabeth Wilberforce, wealthy merchants of Hull. Here, young Wilberforce was surrounded by the smells and sounds of a bustling seaport town until his father died, after which he was sent to live with his uncle and aunt, William and Hannah Wilberforce. At their home, Wilberforce received his first serious religious impressions. Friends of George Whitefield, they laid the basis for Wilberforce's later conversion. It was in their home, too, that Wilberforce met one of the most colorful figures in England, John Newton. Jolly and affectionate, Newton had been a sea captain and a slaver until he turned his life over to Christ. So strong were these Methodist influences on the young boy, that when his unsympathetic mother heard of it she brought him home and transferred him to a school in Pocklington.

At the age of seventeen, Wilberforce entered St. John's College, Cambridge, where he was readily accepted by the sons of the wealthy and powerful. But, unlike many of the rich, fee-paying students, who wasted their time at the university, Wilberforce steered a fairly straight course and kept up with his studies. Soon, a goal began to form in his mind: to become a member of Parliament.

In the winter of 1779 to 1780, Wilberforce could be seen frequently in the House of Commons gallery, watching the debates with his new friend William Pitt. In 1780, not yet twenty-one years old, he decided to stand for one of the two seats from his own hometown of Hull. Spending over eight thousand pounds on the election, and holding ox-roasts for his would-be constituents, Wilberforce garnered the same number of votes as the other two candidates put together. But, it was not a victory won merely by money. His character and good family name had as much to do with it as his wealth (although the wealth was necessary to perform the duties expected of any candidate for the House of Commons). His victory, as one supporter assured him, "indicates your superior pretensions, and confirms the character given of you by our friends."[1]

Wilberforce's first months in Parliament were spent surveying the political landscape and learning the ways of the House. In his spare time, he joined many of London's luxurious clubs where he gambled, joked, drank, and sang. (The Prince of Wales said he would "go anywhere to hear Wilberforce sing.") For the next four years, his career was without any great distinction. He attended Parliament regularly, spoke seldom, and generally voted against the expenditure of money and with his friend Pitt.

A turning point in Wilberforce's career came in 1784, when his plan to represent the largest county in England, York, came to fruition. Speaking at a meeting of freeholders in York just after the government had been dissolved and an election called for, Wilberforce was so well received that the leaders of his York audience cried out, "We'll have this man for our County Member." James Boswell, the famous biographer, was in the crowd and said, "I saw a little fellow on the table speaking—a perfect shrimp. But presently the shrimp swelled into a whale."[2] Wilberforce won the election, gaining not only the title "Knight of the Shire for the County of York" but also the prestige that went with representing England's largest county. In his new position, he gave more and increasingly improved speeches. As a speaker, he had the unique gift of exploring both sides of a question before giving his own opinion. On one occasion, Wilberforce saw both sides of a question so clearly that when he sat down, a Mr. Whitbread jumped up and said, "Mr. Speaker, my Honorable friend who just sat down has as usual spoken on both sides of the Question," at which the House broke into laughter. Of his speaking, Wraxal, in his *Memories*, marveled that such an ugly, undignified little man could speak "with such great perspicuity as well as fluency."[3]

And of course, much of his early political education came from being with Pitt, who was now Prime Minister. In 1748, he wrote:

> For weeks and months together I have spent hours with him every morning while he was transacting business with his secretaries. Hundreds of times, probably, I have called him out

of bed. . . . As he knew I should not ask anything of him, and as he reposed so much confidence in me as to be persuaded that I should
never use any information I might obtain from
him for any unfair purpose, he talked freely
before me of men and things, of actual, medi-
tated or questionable appointments and plans,
projects, speculations, etc., etc.[4]

But, the real turning point of his life was not his
friendship with Pitt, nor his election to represent York.
It was his decision to turn his life over to the Lord
Jesus Christ.

Eternal matters were seemingly the farthest thing
from Wilberforce's mind when he planned a trip to the
Continent. It would be a family party with his mother
and sister and two young ladies who were his relatives.
Almost on impulse, he invited his former tutor, Isaac
Milner, to go along and serve both as tour guide and
traveling companion. They made their way to Nice,
enjoying the warm sunshine and carefree life of English travelers in the south of France. But, a letter from
England interrupted their pleasure. It was Pitt, request-
ing Wilberforce to return home for the opening of the
House of Commons. On the journey home, Wilberforce
had an opportunity to read Phillip Doddridge's book,
The Rise and Progress of Religion in the Soul. Alarmed at
the condition of his own soul, he had long conversa-
tions with Milner. Milner, an Evangelical, convinced
Wilberforce—at least intellectually—that he needed to
confess to Jesus as his Savior and Lord. During a second trip to the Continent with Milner in 1785, intellectual assent grew into conviction. It was probably at this
time that Wilberforce became a Christian.[5]

Since nearly all politicians drank, gambled, and
moved in circles with purely secular interests, Wilberforce
assumed that to become a good Christian he would
have to give up his career. In turmoil, because he loved

politics and was good at it, Wilberforce went to see his boyhood hero, John Newton. Should he give up politics and become one of Wesley's lay preachers? Should he give up life in the city and live a life of prayer and meditation in the country? To which Newton replied: "It is hoped and believed that the Lord has raised you up for the good of the nation."[6] Newton told him that if he stayed in politics he would find opportunities to advance God's kingdom that other men could only dream of. He also advised him to inform the Prime Minister of his change of convictions, for now he could no longer vote a party line if it conflicted with Christian principles. Later, after having told Pitt of his conversion, Wilberforce wrote in his diary: "Pitt tried to reason me out of my convictions, but soon found himself unable to combat their correctness, if Christianity was true. The fact is, he is so absorbed in politics, that he has never given himself time for due reflection on religion."[7]

The change in his behavior and politics was almost immediate. He was no fool; he saw clearly that if a man became a Christian, that fact should influence everything he does. He stopped going to plays and theaters, became more cheerful and less temperamental, and began to base his political opinions upon the Scriptures. He resigned from five clubs in one day. Because the change was so complete, he was accused of going mad. On hearing this charge, one Mrs. Sykes said: "If this is madness, I hope that he will bite us all."[8]

"A man who acts from principles I profess," he told a constituent, "reflects that he is to give an account of his political conduct at the Judgement Seat of Christ."

Like John Newton, he urged converts to remain in their callings—including the Army and Parliament—and use their influence to advance the Gospel. John Pollock has written:

In planning moral reform, he showed aware-
ness that politics are more influenced by the
climate of an age than by the personal piety of
statesmen and politicians. Wilberforce believed,
nonetheless, that England's destiny lay safest in
the hands of men of clear Christian principle,
and that submission to Christ was a man's most
important political as well as religious decision.[9]

One of Wilberforce's first actions as a Christian
was to get the king (George III) to issue a proclamation
calling for spiritual reformation throughout the land.
For better or worse, the king was the head of the
church in England and, according to English custom,
was responsible for making such a call. Thus, on 1 June
1787, George III gazetted a *Proclamation for the Encouragement of Piety and Virtue.*

"Whereas we cannot but observe with inexpress-
ible concern, the rapid progress of impiety and licen-
tiousness," the proclamation read,

and that deluge of profaness, immorality, and
every kind of vice, which, to the scandal of our
holy religion, and to the evil example of our
loving subjects, have broken in upon the nation: we, therefore . . . have thought fit, by the
choice of our Privy Council, to issue this our
loyal Proclamation, and do hereby declare our
Royal Purpose and resolution to discountenance
and punish all manner of vice, profaness and
immorality, in all person, of whatsoever degree
or quality, within this our Realm, and particularly in such as are employed near our Royal
person.[10]

In order to encourage piety and virtue, Wilberforce
urged the creation of a Proclamation Society with local
chapters that would help to encourage virtue and discourage vice. Among other things, this society would
help bring to trial people who defied the laws of the

land. There was a limit, though, in how far the society should go. On numerous occasions, Wilberforce spoke out against using deceit to secure convictions as well as against prosecuting writers and publishers for blasphemy, since experience had shown that legal action helped to advertise such publications and since Christianity only grew stronger from these attacks. Long before Robert Peel, he called for the creation of municipal police forces for the cities to prevent crime. He urged his fellow M.P.s to curtail their activities on Sunday—if not for their consciences, at least for those of their servants, who had no choice but to work on the Lord's Day if their masters decided to go yachting, hunting, or partying. Wilberforce himself set the example: he went to church twice and would only travel or discuss politics in the gravest emergency. Wilberforce, when home, would hold family prayers twice daily. They were generally short, but reverent.[11]

As a member of Parliament, Wilberforce was responsible to both represent and work for the good of the whole British Empire. And, as he surveyed conditions in Britain's vast holdings, he could not help but notice the scourge of slavery. His fellow Evangelicals—John Wesley and John Newton—had spoken out against it. Now, it was his turn.

For a number of years, slavery had been a concern of certain Evangelical preachers, the Quakers, and Granville Sharp, who had led the charge to abolish slavery in Great Britain proper. In 1785, the anti-slavery cause had been given more legitimacy through a pivotal study by Thomas Clarkson entitled *An Essay on Slavery*. Originally a prizewinning essay at Cambridge University, the book had been translated from the original scholarly Latin and published in English. The book was based on extensive interviews with men who knew the slave trade intimately: sailors, ships' doctors, merchants, and traders. In obtaining his information,

Clarkson's life had been in danger. On one occasion, in Liverpool, a gang closed in on him, intending to throw him into the ocean. Clarkson, a powerfully-built man, fought his way loose and was back again the next day to continue his investigation. Having received what he considered to be a call from God, Clarkson dedicated his life to the destruction of the slave trade.

In the summer of 1787, Clarkson set up a Committee for the Abolition of the Slave Trade, with Granville Sharp as its first chairman.

That same year, Wilberforce wore out the pages of his copy of Clarkson's *Essay on Slavery*. Along with his own research, Clarkson's book convinced Wilberforce that he must do something about the slave trade. "As soon as I had arrived thus far in my investigation of the Slave Trade," he would eventually tell the House, "I confess to you, so enormous, so dreadful, so irremediable did its wickedness appear that my own mind was completely made up for Abolition."[12] On Sunday, 28 October 1787, he wrote in his diary, "God Almighty has set before me two great objects, the suppression of the Slave Trade and the Reformation of Manners."[13]

Soon, Wilberforce gathered around himself a group of men dedicated to helping him abolish slavery. Granville Sharp was among them, as was Thomas Clarkson. They also included Zachary Macaulay, a quiet, patient researcher who dug up evidence condemning the slave trade. Eventually, he became a walking encyclopedia. Whenever Wilberforce needed information, he would say, "Let's look it up in Macaulay."[14]

In 1788, before Wilberforce would launch his crusade against slavery, he fell gravely ill. His enemies even made plans to regain his seat in Parliament after his expected demise. But, Wilberforce recovered, and, though not well enough to attend Parliament's sessions, he prevailed upon his friend, William Pitt, to introduce the abolition issue in the House. Basically, the motion bound the House to discuss the issue in a future session. This did little to alarm the West Indies bloc, since they felt that there was little threat in a motion to merely discuss the issue. But, when Sir William Dolben introduced a one-year trial bill to limit the number of slaves transported per ship, the pro-slavery bloc rose up with all its fury. Tales of cruelty were merely fiction, they said; moreover, destruction of the slave trade would destroy "two thirds of the commerce on which this country depends." Enraged by these exaggerations, Pitt joined in the fray and pushed for passage of Dolben's bill, which passed both Houses in June 1788.

The success of Dolben's bill mobilized the pro-slavery forces as never before. Thus, when Wilberforce returned to Parliament, he found the opposition arrayed against him. In his first major speech for abolition, Wilberforce said:

> When I consider the magnitude of the subject which I am to bring before the House—a subject, in which the interest, not of this country, nor of Europe alone, but of the whole world, and of posterity, are involved . . . it is impossible for me not to feel both terrified and concerned at my own inadequacy to such a task. But I march forward with a firm step in full assurance that my cause will bear me out . . . the total abolition of the slave trade. . . .
>
> I mean not to accuse anyone, but to take the shame upon myself, in common, indeed with the whole Parliament of Great Britain, for having suffered this horrid trade to be carried on under their authority. We are all guilty—we ought all to plead guilty, and not exculpate ourselves by throwing the blame on others.[15]

But, Wilberforce's speeches weren't enough to secure passage of Dolben's bill for another year. No more

serious action was taken until April 1791, when a motion
to abolish the slave trade was defeated by 163 to 88.

Realizing that the battle to abolish slavery might
take a lifetime—or several lifetimes—Wilberforce and
his allies began meeting to plot strategy at Henry
Thornton's house in Clapham, four miles south of
Westminster. But, unlike the smoke-filled rooms of later
political causes, these meetings—held in Thornton's
library which had been designed by William Pitt—were
often bathed in prayer. Out of these meetings came
the idea of appealing to the people, to do an "end-run"
around the puppets of the West Indian interests in
Parliament and create a groundswell of support for the
abolition of slavery. "It is on the general impression
and feeling of the nation we must rely . . . so let the
flame be fanned."

Thousands of pamphlets, detailing the evils of slavery, were distributed. Members of the Clapham Sect
spoke at public meetings. Josiah Wedgewood, maker
of famous China, designed a cameo that depicted a
slave kneeling, in bondage, saying, "Am I not a man
and a brother?" William Cowper, the famous
hymnwriter, wrote *The Negro's Complaint*, and thousands of copies were circulated throughout the country:

> Still in thought as free as ever What are
> England's rights, I ask, Me from my delights to
> sever, Me to torture, me to task? Fleecy locks
> and black complexion Cannot forfeit Nature's
> claims; Skins may differ, but affection Dwells in
> black and white the same. Is there, as you some-
> times tell us, Speaking from His throne, the
> sky? Ask Him if your knotted scourges, Fetters,
> blood-extorting screws, Are the means which
> duty urges Agents of His will to use?[16]

Taking their cue from America during the War for
Independence, the abolitionists organized a boycott of

slave-grown sugar, which gained a following of over three hundred thousand people. Just a few days before his death, John Wesley wrote Wilberforce these words of encouragement:

> Unless the divine power has raised you up to be as "Athanasius against the world," I see not how you can go through your glorious enterprise in opposing that execrable villany, which is the scandal of religion, of England, and of human nature. Unless God has raised you up for this very thing, you will be worn out by the opposition of men and devils. But if God be for you, who can be against you? Are all of them stronger than God?
>
> O be not weary of well-doing! Go on, in the name of God and in the power of His might, till even American slaver (the vilest that ever saw the sun) shall vanish away before it.
>
> Reading this morning a tract wrote by a poor African, I was particularly struck by the circumstance, that a man who has a black skin, being wronged or outraged by a white man, can have no redress; it being LAW in all of our colonies that the OATH of a black man against a white man goes for nothing. What villainy is this!
>
> That He who has guided you from youth up may continue to strengthen you in this and all things is the prayer of, dear sir, your affectionate servant, John Wesley.[17]

In 1792, Wilberforce was encouraged by the results of a great parliamentary debate. When Wilberforce finally moved an amendment "That the slave trade ought to be gradually abolished," the amendment was carried by 193 votes to 125. But, that same year, the abolition cause was set back when France declared war on England. Viewing the anarchy brought about by the

French Revolution, many Englishmen feared what might happen if the slaves were freed.

Matters became worse when Wilberforce advocated peace with the radical French, who were wreaking havoc all over Europe. Soon, anyone associated with the abolition movement was referred to as a Jacobin. Each year, Wilberforce introduced a resolution to abolish the slave trade; each year it was defeated. The whole situation changed abruptly when William Pitt died. Pitt's death was a serious personal blow to Wilberforce. During Pitt's last days, Bishop Pretyman kept Wilberforce from discussing eternal matters with Pitt. Pretyman proposed prayer only six hours before his death. Years later, Wilberforce wrote: "I never could forgive his never proposing prayer to our poor old friend Pitt . . . till within six hours before his dissolution." Wilberforce said he wished that "he and I might confer freely on the most important of all subjects."[18]

Although Pitt was not against abolition, the new leadership of Parliament placed the issue higher on the agenda and were willing to try new strategies. In 1807, Prime Minister William Grenville introduced the bill to abolish slavery in the House of Lords first instead of the House of Commons. After a month-long battle, the bill finally passed at four o'clock in the morning, 4 February 1807. On 22 February, the second reading was held in the House.

A new generation of statesmen, influenced by Wilberforce's years of work, rose up to speak in favor of the Bill. At the height of the proceedings, Solicitor-General Romilly swept the House to a pitch of excitement with a passionate tribute to Wilberforce. Contrasting Bonaparte and Wilberforce, Romilly pictured each as he retired for a night's rest: Bonaparte in pomp and power, yet his sleep tormented by the blood he had spilt; Wilberforce, on the other hand, returning after the vote that night "into the bosom of his happy and delighted family to lie down in perfect peace, conscious of having preserved so many millions of his fellow creatures." Above the roar of "hear, hear," came three cheers for Wilberforce. Wilberforce sat bent in his chair, his head in his hands, tears streaming down his face. A few hours later, the motion to abolish the slave trade (not slavery) carried by a vote of 283 to 16. "No one expected this great question to be carried with so high a hand," wrote Richard Ryder, an M.P. "No one is more surprised than Wilberforce himself. He attributes it to the immediate interposition of Providence." In the celebration that followed, Wilberforce turned to his friend Henry Thornton and asked, "Well, Henry, what shall we abolish next?"[19]

For the next eighteen years, Wilberforce worked for the total emancipation of existing slaves, until his retirement in 1825. In 1812, he resigned his Yorkshire seat and its many responsibilities and accepted from Lord Calthorpe the pocket borough of Bramber, near the Sussex coast. Not only was his health at risk, but he wanted to spend more time with his family. Like all good leaders, he began grooming younger men to take his place as the leaders of abolitionists. In 1821, he wrote to Thomas Fowell Buxton, inviting him to lead "this holy enterprise," as he called the abolition campaign. Buxton accepted, and with Wilberforce as his guide he learned the business of leading the abolitionists. It was under the leadership of Buxton and the M.P.s whose sentiments had been formed by Wilberforce that all slavery was abolished in 1833.

The abolition of slavery in the British Empire was the great end of Wilberforce's life, but it was by no means the only object.

In Parliament, he advanced many causes which he associated with a Christian view of politics. He sought to stop the burning of women convicts, considering it cruel and unusual punishment. (Female convicts were hanged first, but could be burned alive if the hangman was inept.) He supported the Combination Acts in 1799 which kept workers from combining against their employers. For Wilberforce, the Combination Acts were passed in defense of the realm and did not represent economic repression. He supported union with Ireland and admission of Catholics to Parliament if it would solve the Irish question.

He could act independently of his constituents if he felt it was best for the whole realm: on one occasion he supported the Irish Propositions to help Ireland even though his West Riding woolen manufacturer constituents believed it would help Irish textile manufacturers at their expense. Although he supported laws allowing for the creation of mechanized mills— Wilberforce was in on the ground floor of modern capitalism and the Industrial Revolution—he also made certain that the bill would not kill domestic weaving. In his view, cottage industry insured that small weavers could continue to work either when factories could not or when workers might be laid-off from the factories. He embraced Adam Smith's basic principles but did not follow him in all his thinking.

One of his great blunders was his support of the Corn Laws of 1815, which stated that no foreign corn could be imported until the price of homegrown corn (all grain) had reached a certain level. The result was shortages of bread and near starvation in parts of England.[20] In his defense, the principles of free trade were still being hammered out and were not clearly understood; even Adam Smith never understood what gave something value—that discovery would have to wait until the Austrian economists came along. And, he also wanted the fixed price to be lower than that set by Parliament. Nevertheless, the Corn Laws were a bad policy and their abolition years later paved the way for one of the greatest periods of free trade in history as well as Britain's vast wealth.

In matters of religion, Wilberforce sought no particular help from government to advance evangelical Christianity, although he wanted the government to enforce the laws. One historian says, "He held that Roman religion was in error, and opposed the grant to Maynorth College for the training of priests and would have welcomed Ireland's conversion to Protestantism; but he held an even lower opinion of 'political' Protestants, men who had no religion yet belabored the Roman Catholics for political ends."[21] In 1813, he worked against penal statutes in matters of religion.

The East India Company had been given a virtual carte blanche in India but didn't want anything to do with spreading Christianity for fear it might cause an upheaval and then hinder commerce. Since the East India Company had been given a monopoly by Parliament, Wilberforce reasoned, it was up to Parliament to address the problem and give free reign to missionaries and chaplains from England. "You will know," he wrote on 14 April 1806, "how deeply I feel on the subject, when I frankly confess to your Lordship that next to slave trade, I have long thought our making no effort to introduce the blessings of religion and moral improvement among our subjects in the East, the greatest of our national crimes."[22] Wilberforce fought for a new East India Company Charter that would permit the activity of missionaries, ordained or lay, Established or Dissenter. "Really, we have too many in both houses who seem to think our dominions safer under Brahma and Vishnu, than under that of the Almighty."[23]

Wilberforce's concern strikes home today, when many in the West have succumbed to a missionary movement from the East—under the guise of the New Age Movement, Transcendental Meditation, and the philosophy of Gandhi (the Indian government spent millions on the movie *Gandhi* to promote state Hinduism).[24]

Wilberforce's answer to the power of Hinduism, then and now, was Christianity. In a 22 June 1813 speech, Wilberforce showed the ill effects of Hinduism. Those effects included a disdain for relieving human suffering (such suffering is a necessary part of Karma), the practice of suttee, or wife destruction, a lack of political and economic freedom due to the caste system, and widespread starvation. What was the remedy? "That remedy, Sir," Wilberforce concluded,

> is Christianity, which I justly call the appropriate remedy; for Christianity then assumes her true character ... when she takes under her protection those poor degraded beings on whom philosophy looks down with disdain or perhaps with contemptuous condescension. On the very first promulgation of Christianity it was declared by its great Author as "Glad tidings to the poor," and, ever faithful to her character, Christianity still delights to instruct the ignorant, to succor the needy, to comfort the sorrowful, to visit the forsaken.[25]

He rejected the charge that he was advocating compulsory conversion to Christianity.

> Compulsion and Christianity! Why the very terms are at variance with each other—the ideas are incompatible. In the language of Inspiration itself, Christianity has been called the "law of liberty." Her service in the excellent formularies of our church has been truly denominated "perfect freedom"; and they, let me add, will most advance her cause who contend for it in her own spirit of character.[26]

He was not asking Parliament to ordain evangelism, but merely to tolerate it. Such a free exchange of ideas and beliefs is one of the hallmarks of a free society. In 1813, owing to Wilberforce's leadership, the new East India Charter guaranteed liberty to propagate the Christian faith.

Although the government could free the slaves, since it was the government which protected the slave trader and his trade, Wilberforce knew that government could not, indeed should not, do everything. The Bible expressly stated, in Romans 13, that government's role was limited. Therefore, if he wanted to advance the Christian faith, much of it had to be done outside the sphere of government.

While waiting for Parliament to outlaw slavery, Wilberforce joined with others to create a British colony in Africa for freed slaves. This colony, to be called Sierra Leone, would give England's poor blacks (mostly newly freed blacks) a new start in life. Unfortunately, the colony was never really successful.

Many other Christian endeavors were begun by Wilberforce. "Factories did not spring up more rapidly in Leeds and Manchester than schemes of benevolence beneath his roof," wrote James Stephen about Wilberforce.[27] And, of course, benevolence in Wilberforce's book was centered around the spread of the Gospel. He sent missionaries to Tahiti and subscribed to the new Baptist Missionary Society, which sent out William Carey. He helped form the Society for the Better Observance of Sunday, as well as the British and Foreign Bible Society. This latter organization was the only religious organization uniting Churchmen and Dissenters. Previous to founding the British and Foreign Bible Society, he had supported a small Bible society that gave Bibles to soldiers and sailors.[28]

These were but a few of Wilberforce's charities. He did much more helping people on an individual basis, giving out money as freely as advice to the many people that sought him out. When Charles Wesley died and his widow needed aid, Wilberforce gave her an annual allowance until her death. He made himself available to thousands more through his book, *A Practical View of the Prevailing Religious System of Professed Christians, in the Higher and Middle Classes in This Country, Contrasted with Real Christianity*. Published on 12 April 1797, it became a best-seller. Years later, the great Thomas Chalmers, founder of the Free Church of Scotland, acknowledged that Wilberforce's *Practical View* helped bring him into a genuine and personal experience of salvation.[29]

In his personal life, Wilberforce was as devoted a husband as he was a Christian. He married Barbara Ann Spooner, who, like most of those close to Wilberforce (except his mother) called him Wilber. Eventually, they had four sons and two daughters. He led his family in prayer and in morning and evening devotions, in addition to his own private devotions. Each day he got up at seven o'clock to spend the first hour of the day in prayer and Bible study. "In the calmness of the morning," he wrote, "before the mind is heated and wearied by the turmoil of the day, you have a season of unusual importance for communion with God and with yourself."

Like most politicians, Wilberforce could not help but get involved in controversy, in problems to which there were no satisfactory solutions. Such was the case with the "Trial of Queen Caroline."

In 1820, King George III died and was succeeded by George IV, a timid, petulant, and highly unpopular ruler. Much of the animosity of liberals, radicals, and the common man against things such as the Corn Laws, the so-called Peterloo massacre (in which several people were killed during a political rally asking for parliamentary reform) and the reactionary legislation that followed was concentrated on him. In 1820, this hostility was given a new focus when the king forced his ministers to introduce a bill in Parliament divorcing him from his wife, Caroline of Brunswick, who had allegedly committed adultery on the Continent. When Caroline returned to claim her rights as queen, the liberals, radicals, and much of the citizenry rallied around her in her role as the injured wife. The crisis was so great that it threatened to bring down the government, including the monarchy.[30]

Because of his moral stature as both a Christian and an Independent, Wilberforce was called on to mediate. Through a series of negotiations, Wilberforce tried to avoid a divorce, yet get the queen to leave the public scene. The negotiations went along well until they got stuck on the question of the State Prayers. The king insisted that her name be struck from the Liturgy, while she insisted that it remain. Wilberforce cut a deal with the queen, based on a note from her advisor Brougham, that she would indeed allow for her name to be dropped if the House of Commons gave her a "recommendation to any Court on the Continent."

But, when Wilberforce presented the compromise, which he thought she had approved of, the queen refused to let her name be dropped. The result was the long, drawn-out "Trial of Queen Caroline." Wilberforce never mentioned the note from Brougham, making it look like the compromise was his scheme and that he was little more than a meddler and a puppet of the king. "What a lesson it is to a man," he wrote, "not to set his heart on low popularity when after 40 years disinterested public service I'm believed by the Bulk to be a Hypocritical Rascal. O what a comfort it is to have to fly for refuge to a God of unchangeable truth and love."[31] The issue was finally solved and the nation saved by a Higher Tribunal: Queen Caroline died unexpectedly in 1821.

In 1833, Wilberforce's health failed. By June his knees and thighs were swelling. Each morning he was taken outside in a wheelchair for fresh air. By mid-July, he seemed to be getting better. Late on Friday, 26 July, he heard that the Abolition of Slavery had passed its third reading in the Commons. Passage through the Lords being not in doubt, slavery as a legal state was to all intents dead. "Thank God that I have lived to witness a day in which England is willing to give twenty millions sterling for the Abolition of Slavery," he exclaimed.

It seemed as if Wilberforce had been waiting to receive the news, for on Saturday his health declined dramatically. By three o'clock Monday morning, 29 July, he was with the Lord. Thus passed from the scene one of history's greatest Christian statesmen—a man whose life not only helped to free the slaves, but also set the moral tone for Victorian England.

Chapter Eight

Sir Robert Anderson: Christian Civil Servant

Sir Robert Anderson never ran for public office, never debated in a Parliament or Congress. Yet, through most of his life, he worked for the government—in civil service, in police work, and on several royal commissions—without compromising his testimony as a Christian. As such, he serves as an example of what the Christian in government service should be.

Sir Robert Anderson has gone down in the annals of crime-fighting as one of Scotland Yard's greatest detectives. In a long career of service under Her Majesty, Queen Victoria, Anderson helped to avert several plots to overthrow the British government in Ireland, as well as an attempt on the queen herself. His writings on crime are still valid for today. Anderson's greatest contribution to crime-fighting came not so much in apprehending criminals as in attacking sin at its very root, for, between public duties, Anderson spent his time preaching, passing out tracts, and writing books explaining and defending the Christian faith.

Born in Dublin of Ulster stock from a long line of public servants, Anderson became a born-again Christian in the revivals of 1859 and 1860. Having been trained as a lawyer, Anderson had been skeptical of the claims of the Gospel. After all, the differences in the four Gospels showed that they could not have been divinely inspired—or so he thought. But, then, one day he heard an address on the Gospels in a friend's drawing room. In a rapid summary of the Gospels, the speaker showed how each one was written for a specific purpose and to a specific audience in the ancient world. "Light shone on the Book where all had been doubt and darkness," Anderson later wrote, "and I learned that while I boasted of being a superior person and a critic, I was but a poor conceited ignoramus."[1]

Ultimately, his conversion came after hearing a message by Dr. John Hall. Nearly fifty years later, Anderson recorded his testimony:

> Until I get to Heaven, I shall never know whether I was not a child of God in infancy. My mother regarded me as God-given to take the place of a son who died shortly before I was born, and who was evidently a veritable Timothy. She loved to talk to me about him, and his story had a great influence upon me. Even in early years prayer was no mere form with me, and I delighted in reading the Gospel of John and some favourite Psalms. But in due course I was taught that no one who has not been "converted" can be a child of God, and I had never experienced any crisis of that kind.
>
> As time went by my conviction deepened that I had not been "converted." But owing doubtless to my early experience and to the restraints of a Christian home I continued to lead "a religious life." And I had occasional fits of penitence and anxiety. But they were transient; and their after-effect was to make me increasingly callous, the hardening process being intensified by the influence of that other doctrine that my eternal destiny depended entirely on whether I was "elect," and therefore nothing I could do would affect the issue.

Such was my condition in 1860. But in that memorable year of Revival new spiritual longings were awakened in me by the conversion of one of my sisters through attending services which J. Denham Smith was holding in Dublin. Owing, however, to my experience of such periods of anxiety I refused even to acknowledge a desire to go to a meeting. But on a certain evening when my sister very specially wished to be present her promised escort failed, and I got credit for unselfish kindness by offering to accompany her. The meeting only disappointed and vexed me. The sermon brought no comfort and some of the hymns offended me; for, owing possibly to my being ecclesiastically Scottish, certain popular hymns do not suit my spiritual digestion.

The fact of my sister's conversion still held me, however, and I cherished the thought that the next Sunday services in the Kirk might bring me blessing. But the morning service left me more discouraged than ever; and I made up my mind that if the evening one brought no relief I would give up the quest, and seek to enjoy life again as best I could.

The evening preacher was Dr. John Hall, afterwards of New York. His sermon was a type to which we are now accustomed, for he boldly proclaimed forgiveness of sins and eternal life as God's gift in grace, unreserved and unconditional, to be received as we sat in the pews. His sermon thrilled me. Yet I deemed his doctrine unscriptural, so I waylaid him as he left the vestry and on our homeward way tackled him about his "heresies."

My first point was that he had no warrant for saying that there was forgiveness for sinners without first ascertaining whether they had re-

pented. This he met by quoting Scripture to
prove that repentance was not contrition; nor
was it a work preparatory to coming to Christ,
but a change produced by believing the Gospel
as the Word of God. . . . At last he let go my
arm, and facing me as we stood upon the pave-
ment he repeated with great solemnity his
message and appeal: "I tell you as a minister of
Christ and in His name that there is life for you
here and now if you will accept Him. Will you
accept Christ or will you reject Him?" After a
pause—how prolonged I know not—I exclaimed,
"In God's name I will accept Christ." Not another word passed between us, but after another pause he wrung my hand and left me.
And I turned homeward with the peace of God
filling my heart.[2]

It was not long after his conversion that he became
committed to personal work, a commitment that only
deepened as he grew older. One of his first endeavors
was to go on what Christians in his day called com-
mando raids—sudden incursions of two or three laymen into towns deep inside Ireland with the sole purpose of proclaiming the Gospel. Sometimes local Anglican ministers cooperated with them; at other times
the churches were closed to them, just as they were in
the days of Wesley and Whitefield. But, just as in
Wesley's day, Anderson and his fellow "commandos"
preached in the open air.

In 1862, Anderson took his law degree from Trinity College, Dublin. When not preaching or leading a
Bible study, Anderson earned his living by practicing
law. In 1865, he entered the Secret Service when government officials asked him to prepare a summary of
all the papers at Dublin Castle that dealt with the Fenian
Society. (The Fenian Society had been founded to
overthrow the British government in Ireland, using

force if necessary.) The result was a book on the Fenian Movement that later proved valuable to the police.

Soon he was working full time for the British Secret Service. Making contacts with prisoners and other possible informants, Anderson was able to keep track of many of the Fenian leaders both in Ireland and America. By keeping several Fenian leaders in his pay as informants, he was able to work behind the scenes to prevent many crimes from being committed. "I will only add that the hold thus obtained upon the organization," Anderson later wrote, "prevented the commission of outrages at a critical time, and further that the information received from these men was never used to bring a criminal charge against any member of the conspiracy."[3]

Keeping the name of one of his informants in America secret for over twenty-one years, he was criticized by certain politicians for refusing to reveal his name. "Anderson's idea of secrecy is not to tell the Secretary of State," remarked Sir William Harcort. Later, Anderson told his son why he felt his actions were justified: his first Fenian informant was shot as a result of his name being given to Lord Mayo, then Chief Secretary for Ireland. When Lord Mayo passed the name on to the Lord-lieutenant of Ireland, it was overheard by some servants, who passed it on to a Fenian sympathizer. Not long after, the informant was found dead, with a hole in his head.[4]

Various comments by Anderson reveal that as a Christian he wrestled with being in this "cloak and dagger" business. "Such work was never to my taste," he wrote.[5] Yet, Anderson saw the need for undercover work in this less-than-perfect world. He viewed himself not so much as a spy but simply as a policeman and took comfort in the fact that he was undertaking defensive measures to protect the innocent.

For Anderson, the world of espionage was not a shadow-world where no morals applied. Good was good, and evil was evil. He was on the side of good, and it was his job to root out evil and destroy it before it had a chance to strike. He avoided lies and deception simply by keeping quiet. A good Englishman, he kept a stiff upper lip, and he kept both lips closed. It was a case of discretion preserving both his professional life as well as his Christian testimony. One of his top agents wrote of Anderson:

> He never wavered or grew lax in his care. He proved indeed to me not the ordinary official superior, but a kind, trusty friend and adviser, ever watchful in my interests, ever sympathizing with my danger and difficulties. To him and to him alone was I known as a Secret Service agent during the whole of the 21 years of which I speak. Therein lay the secret of my safety. If others less worthy of this trust had been charge with the knowledge of my identity, then I fear I should not be here on English soil quietly penning these lines.[6]

More than one former British agent was able to spend his retirement years tending an English country garden under an English heaven because of Anderson's discretion. Serving God and country, Anderson kept the names and activities of his agents secret for many years, often at the peril of his own career and safety.

Sir Robert Anderson despised the political decisions which let criminals go free: "Such are our ways with dynamiters," he wrote, "these men were aliens who came in time of peace to perpetrate outrages which if committed by soldiers in war-time would ensure them short shrift after trial by drumhead court-martial. . . . And yet these miscreants were treated with a quixotic leniency."[7]

When Anderson first took up work with the Civil Service in 1877, he was told that the way to succeed is to do as little as possible as quietly as possible. As a Christian, Anderson refused, worked diligently instead, and through his efforts helped to mold the modern British police force.

In 1888, Anderson was asked to take over the Criminal Investigation Department of Scotland Yard. (Scotland Yard had received its name from the fact that it had been located in the area where Scottish kings stayed while visiting London.) The night before he took office, the second of the infamous Jack the Ripper murders took place. His charge from the Home Secretary: "We hold you responsible to find the murderer." Anderson was convinced that they had found the murderer; unfortunately, the only witness refused to testify in court. According to Anderson, the Ripper was an East European who died in an asylum.[8] Knowing that the public was safe, Anderson took the case no further.

During these years, under Anderson's leadership, Scotland Yard became world famous. Sir John Maylan wrote of Scotland Yard and the Metropolitan Police:

> The period 1890 to 1900 proved to be one during which there was almost continuous decrease in crime. . . . By signal successes in sensational murder cases such as that of Neil Cream the poisoner, and Milsom and Fowler the Muswell Hill Murderers, and by steady achievement in the less advertised everyday business of dealing with rogues in general, the C.I.D. built up in the "nineties" a world-wide reputation for efficiency in crime detection. Crime reached a low watermark in 1899.

Characteristically, Anderson attributed his success not to himself but to his men:

It is to the habit of dealing with criminals instead of with crime that the phenomenal success of the C.I.D. is largely due. I have no reserve in praising a department of which I was
recently Chief, and for the excellent reason that
no one knows better than I do to whom the
praise for that success is due. With a chief who
did not enjoy the fullest confidence and respect
of his subordinates success would be impossible.
But the best of chiefs can do little more than
stand behind the working staff—a body of officers that as a body when judged by the double
test of efficiency and character are unequalled
in the world. Character I include with emphasis
because it is often overlooked when judging the
relative merits of different forces.[9]

One of Anderson's techniques in solving crimes
was to round up the possible suspects and use the
process of elimination to find the perpetrator. The
more serious the crime, the greater the possibility it
was committed by a professional criminal. "Great crimes
are the work of great criminals," he once said, "and
great criminals are very few."[10]

On one occasion, he became convinced more than
ever that most crimes are committed by professionals:
he had locked himself out of his own house, and it
took him the better part of an hour to get in. Thus, he
concluded that most burglaries were committed by men
who are burglars, in the sense that other men are
doctors, lawyers, architects, etc.[11]

When John O'London asked Anderson what he
thought of Sir Arthur Conan Doyle's Sherlock Holmes,
Anderson said:

The inventor of a detective story makes both
the lock and the key, whereas Scotland Yard is
limited to finding the key to the lock. . . . In the
detective story we are interested from first to

last in the solution of the mystery; that solution
is the detective's triumph. . . . But in real life
the elucidation of the mystery is only the first
chapter; if there is no second there is no story
and no triumph.[12]

Beginning in 1891, Anderson began writing a series of articles, published in various journals, that eventually formed a book, published in 1907 as *Criminals
and Crime.*

"We justly deplore the barbarity with which past
generations treated their criminals," Anderson wrote
in the introduction, "the elaborate folly of our present
methods will excite the wonder of generations to come."
Anderson's thesis was that there were two kinds of
criminals: those who fell into crime because of their
disadvantaged upbringing, those who chose a life of
crime as a career and went back to it even after years
of incarceration. With education and a short punishment, the first class of criminals could be reformed.
The second class needed more severe punishment; too
liberal policies which freed unreformed and
unrepentant criminals resulted in a rise in crime and
a decrease in public safety. Such a criminal would be
arrested and sentenced to perhaps five years penal
servitude. Less than four years later he would be back
on the streets practicing his profession. After another
string of crimes, while enjoying a good time, he would
be caught again, and the same farce would be enacted.
Anderson called this routine the "shot drill of the
Criminal Investigation Department," referring to the
obsolete punishment of having inmates carry cannon-
balls from one spot to another in a prison yard and
then carry them back again. Anderson regarded it as a
crime that the energies of the most highly trained police
force in Europe were wasted in exercises like this.

If the sick were treated with the folly which
marks our dealing with criminals, a man with a

violent cough would be sent to the hospital
though possibly suffering from nothing worse
than a fly in his throat or a common cold, whilst
a slight cough would be neglected although it
might be a symptom of some fatal disease.[13]

In order to deal with these professional criminals,
Anderson suggested that repeat offenders be further
charged with being a "professional criminal" and their
prison sentences lengthened. In a lecture he said:

> I do not mean that these men [the professional
> criminals] are to be numbered by tens of thou-
> sands, but they are to be numbered only by
> hundreds. We have in London five hundred
> burglaries a year. . . . they would be the work
> of probably not more than fifty men. What an
> outrage that these fifty professional burglars,
> who are perfectly well known to Scotland Yard,
> should be permitted to be at large, a terror to
> the community.[14]

With regard to armed burglars, he said that if a thief
is found with a revolver he should be given a life sen-
tence.

First offenders and debtors should have short sentences with some offenses being punished by quick
corporal punishment. Although seemingly barbaric, a
few lashes would deter further crime and avoid lengthy
stays in prison. All classes of criminals should have to
work to help make prisons self-supporting. Moreover,
there should be opportunity for mental and moral
improvement, including church services and Bible studies:

> It is nothing short of a scandal, that in a Chris-
> tian and Protestant country the inmates of our
> gaols should know nothing of religion save what
> comes to them officially like the water and the
> gas. To turn from the soul to the intellect; what

means are now available to develop or excite a prisoner's mental powers? Short-sentence prisoners have practically nothing. And the only provision for those who are committed for longer terms is that the use of library books is allowed as a reward for good conduct. But what use would it be to Bill Sykes or to Hodge if you gave him all the thirty-five volumes of Wisdom while you wait! Why should not prisoners on one night a week have a religious meeting of a kind fitted to win them, and on another night a popular lecture calculated to interest and instruct them? By all means make them work hard; and punish severely for idleness or misconduct; but don't starve either their souls or their brains.[15]

Anderson said that the restitution of stolen property ought to be insisted on, and a burglar should not be set at liberty until he had disclosed what he did with the loot.

Anderson was attacked by some as being too hard on criminals, especially by organizations that championed criminals' rights. Speaking of one of these organizations after it had attacked him, he said, "Never a day passes in which the much-maligned police do not give more help to weak and deserving criminals than this sort of society has rendered during all its history."

Ultimately, Anderson knew that the only way to prevent crime was not in better police forces or penal reforms, but a change in the hearts of the people. Such a change could only come through the Gospel of Jesus Christ. A case in point was Wales, which in the early 1900s enjoyed the effects of a great revival, led by Evans Roberts. Taverns closed down, longstanding debts were paid, crime decreased dramatically and there was so little work for the police to do they formed a men's singing group and performed in churches. Cursing and profanity were so diminished that it was reported that a strike was provoked in the coal mines—not by the miners, but by the pitponies which pulled the coal trucks. So many men had given up cursing and profanity that the ponies no longer understood the commands.

Anderson did his part in promoting revival by passing out tracts, preaching, and writing Christian books. He became a frequent speaker at Rescue Missions all across England. His messages were especially blessed by God. One poor woman wrote: "Oh, I could have thrown myself at dear Dr. Anderson's feet and told him what my precious Saviour has done for me. It seemed as if every word he uttered was for me, for me." Eventually, Sir Robert was regarded as one of the great lay preachers of his day—no mean task in an age of great pulpiteers like Charles Haddon Spurgeon, F.B. Meyer, Dwight L. Moody, and Thomas Chalmers.

In order to answer the Higher Critics in Germany, Anderson wrote what would become the first of many helpful books, *Daniel in the Critic's Den*. In order to discredit the prophecies as well as the integrity of Daniel, the Higher Critics proposed a much later date for the writing of Daniel. But, Anderson countered that there were many types of experts and that all testimony should be in before a verdict is made. Speaking as a lawyer, he told them that they could not serve as witness, jury, judge, and executioner all in one. As to the critics' contention that there was no unity in Scripture, Anderson wrote, "These critics are like men who empty the works of a watch into a bowl, and then after examining them in detail arrive at the sapient conclusion that they present no proof of unity of design."

Many other helpful books flowed from his pen— books like *The Silence of God,* which put tragedies like the Armenian massacres into perspective; *Human Destiny*, a book about the afterlife, which Charles Haddon

Spurgeon called "the most valuable contribution on the subject" that he had ever seen; *The Coming Prince*, which set forth the explanation of Daniel's "Seventy Weeks"; and *The Honor of His Name*, which was a plea for reverence in naming the Lord Jesus Christ. Someone who read this last book, Mrs. Duncan Davidson, wrote: "Of all the things I learned from him, I think his holy reverence for his beloved Lord stands out above everything." Many others—reaching into the millions all over the world—benefited from his writings, writings that encouraged Christians and laid waste the theories of the modern skeptics. Dr. James Gray, president of Moody Bible Institute in Chicago, wrote from the "city with big shoulders":

> Sir Robert Anderson is in some respects the most remarkable of current writers on religious subjects, whether we consider his personal history or the range and character of his work. . . . To sit at the feet of a man with such knowledge, mental power, courage and native wit, who is at the same time Spirit-taught, is for the true Christian one of the greatest privileges.

Writing from the South African outback, an upcountry trader wrote: "Sir Robert Anderson's books have put me right. I have thanked God for him many times." In California, a lawyer, at first an atheist, became a Christian after reading *The Silence of God*. Another admiring Christian lawyer said, "Sir Robert holds a brief for Christ."[16]

Sir Robert Anderson died on 15 November 1918, leaving behind his wife, Lady Agnes Anderson, and five fine children. But, he also left behind something else—a model life from which all Christians may learn. He was never ordained as a minister, nor did he hold sway from a regular pulpit each week. Yet, he accomplished far more than many full-time Christian work-

ers. As a Christian detective, he witnessed to many
people who otherwise would have never heard the
Gospel. As a writer on theology, he approached his
subject with the unique perspective of a trained legal
mind. He showed that a Christian could be in the
world, but not of it, as he helped people not only in
this life, but helped them into the life to come. He was,
without a doubt, one of the greatest Christian laymen
of the nineteenth century—an exemplar of a Christian
in government service.

Chapter Nine

Abraham Kuyper:
Prime Minister of Holland

The Dutch have taken it on the chin for a long time. A "Dutch treat" is no treat at all; a "Dutch concert" is a musical horror; and your "Dutch uncle" is the one who speaks with a little too much frankness. These anti-Dutch sentiments which have become part of our language have their origin in the Anglo-Dutch wars of the 1600s. The Dutch deserve much better.

During their long battle with the sea, the Dutch found time to give the world tulips, Santa Claus, waffles, and sauerkraut. To America, they contributed Easter eggs, sleighing, skating, and a host of "vans" and "velts" who helped to build the nation.

But, one of Holland's greatest contributions has to be the life of a thoroughly Christian politician, Abraham Kuyper, who ultimately became that nation's Prime Minister. A Christian first and a politician second, Kuyper's purpose in life was to proclaim "the crown rights of King Jesus over all creation."

Abraham Kuyper was born on Sunday, 29 October 1837, to the Reverend and Mrs. J.F. Kuyper in the fishing village of Maassluis.[1] Their third child and first son, he was named Abraham for his paternal grandfather. Here, in Maassluis, the young Kuyper lived until his father was called to a new pastorate at the

Middleburg State Church. It was in Middleburg, the
capital and chief city of Zeeland province, that Kuyper
spent the major part of his boyhood.

In addition to the opportunities afforded by
Middleburg's fine harbor, sand dunes, streets, and fields,
Kuyper found plenty of stimulation for his curious
intellect. In fact, he never attended grammar school,
having been completely home-schooled. One of the
earliest loves of this future dean of Dutch journalists
was newspaper-reading. Although pleased with his son's
precociousness, father Kuyper was not so sure it was
good for the boy's soul.

"Bram," he finally said, "I don't want you to look
into any papers. They aren't good for you. There's
much better reading matter for a boy your age."[2] Despite his father's admonition, Kuyper loved reading
about current events and would read *De Opregte
Haarlemmer* whenever the opportunity arose. It was an
unusual temptation for a ten year old. Already, the
future editor was interested in the journalist's craft.
Kuyper's childhood dream, however, was not to be a
poet, an editor, or a statesman, but a sailor.

In the spring of 1849, the elder Kuyper received a
call from a church in Leiden, which he accepted. Leiden
was a commercial city with a great university, one that
had been founded by William the Silent as a gift to the
town for their heroic resistance against the Spanish.
Soon after they arrived, Kuyper was placed in an elementary school which prepared its students for the
university.

Kuyper soon discovered that his parents had taught
him so well that he was at the top of his class. Graduating on 6 September 1855, at the age of eighteen,
Kuyper enrolled at Leiden University. Here, Kuyper
reveled in scholarship and study, often studying until
two o'clock in the morning. To train his mind as well
as his oratorical powers, he memorized long poems

and recited them at home in his stentorian voice. To finance his studies, on the side he tutored fellow students. This increased his own store of knowledge, for as all educators know, the best way to learn something for yourself is to teach it to someone else.

Unfortunately, as has been true of so many students both before and after Kuyper, it was at the university that Kuyper lost whatever childhood faith he had. "I entered the university a young man of orthodox faith," he later wrote, "but I had not been in school more than a year and a half before my thought processes had been transformed into the starkest intellectual rationalism."[3]

Leiden, like Holland's other two universities, had ties to the state church that went back hundreds of years. It was a state school connected with a state church. Thus, as both the church and state became increasingly secular, so did the universities. Modernism became the prevailing philosophy, promoted by courtesy of the Dutch taxpayer and by the man in the pew of the state church. It was a real Dutch treat. Captivated by the soul-killing philosophy of Modernism, Kuyper seemed destined to make little impact for the Lord. He had gone over to the enemy's camp.

Despite the fact that he had become a liberal, Kuyper still resolved to prepare for the ministry. Even though he had rejected orthodoxy, he could still use the office of a minister to promote humanitarianism and pursue his scholarly interests. How far Kuyper fell away from the faith could be seen in his reaction to one of Professor L.W. Rauwenhoff's lectures: when Rauwenhoff declared that he could no longer accept Jesus' bodily resurrection as a historical fact, all the students applauded—Kuyper included.[4]

On 20 September 1862, Leiden University conferred on Kuyper the doctor of theology degree. Shortly thereafter, he took on two new responsibilities: his first pastorate, in the state church in the village of Beesd, and a wife, the former Miss Johanna Heudrika Schaay of Rotterdam.

Kuyper arrived in Beesd on 9 August 1863. If he thought he would be able to preach a watered-down Gospel to a congregation of ignorant farmers and tradesmen, he was mistaken. True, his hearers weren't university graduates, and none was so well read as their young pastor. But, there were some orthodox Christians among them, and that made all the difference. True to the faith of the Dutch Reformers, these conservative parishioners relied not so much upon intellectual argument as they did upon living a holy life. As a result, they won Kuyper over to true Christianity, as Kuyper later acknowledged:

> Their conversation was not limited to the affairs of the village. They had interest in spiritual matters. Above all they knew something. I could not measure my impoverished Bible knowledge, the fruit of university study, with that of these plain people. And not only in Bible knowledge. They had a consistent view of life.

> But what drew me most to them was that here the heart spoke—there was inner experience. I came back to them again and again. True, I did my best to function as parson but found that I had more inclination to listen than to teach. After these contacts the Sunday sermons went better. But what vexed me most was their uncompromising spirit. Budge they would not, not an inch. I found myself ever at the fork of the way. Either must I take sharp position against them or go with them without conditions, putting myself under sovereign grace. I thank God that I did not oppose them. Their persistence brought blessing to my heart and the dawn of the Morning Star in my life.[5]

Perhaps the most influential of the simple yet pious folk at the Beesd Church was a young woman by the name of Pietronella Baltus. A spinster in her early thirties, Baltus was the local miller's daughter. A woman of strong conviction, at first she would have nothing to do with the new minister. Finally, one of her neighbors said to her, "The minister is visiting the people in our neighborhood and will probably soon come to see you." To which Baltus replied, "I'll have nothing to do with that man."

"But don't forget, Pietronella," the other said, "that our pastor, too, is traveling to eternity."⁶

That was enough to change Baltus' attitude. Over the succeeding months, Kuyper spent more and more time with the simple peasant woman, discussing the great issues of life. Kuyper found that the answers to these questions were found in the Bible, not in the books of the Modernists. Under the influence of Baltus and other sincere Christians, Kuyper himself became a Christian. It was the turning point of his life; henceforth, to apply the Christian faith to all of life, including politics, became his consuming passion. Years later, he said, "The dream was over. The reality was a world in need of Christ."⁷

In 1867, Kuyper responded to a call to serve a church in Utrecht. Already a project was beginning to form in Kuyper's mind—the reformation of the whole Dutch church—a project that could be better carried out from a strategic pulpit in a large city like Utrecht. Baltus and other Reformed Christians were sorry to see Kuyper go, but they knew that he was marked for leadership and that he needed more room. On 3 November 1867, Kuyper spent his last Sunday in the town where he had found the Lord.

The next two years saw Kuyper lay the foundation for his life's work. As a pastor in Utrecht, he preached "the whole counsel of God" to capacity crowds. The year 1869 was a watershed. First, he declared his interest in politics and its potential for advancing Christianity. "Politicophobia is not Calvinistic, is not Christian, is not ethical," he wrote and joined the Utrecht Anti-Revolutionary Voters Club. He began editing the weekly *De Heraut* and spoke out in favor of Christian schools and against the growing liberal control of the state church. But, most of all, he met Guillaume Groen van Prinsterer, Holland's greatest conservative, Christian historian, and statesman. Of his meeting with Groen, Kuyper wrote:

> . . . till May 18, 1869, when in the consistory room of the Utrecht Cathedral Church on an unforgettable evening I for the first time met the man who by the steadfast look in his eyes and by his earnest, trenchant words at once took such a strong hold on me and so profoundly impressed me that from that hour I became his spiritual associate, no, more, his spiritual son.[8]

Groen, in turn, pointed to Kuyper as the future leader of the Anti-Revolutionary party, which he had founded.

In order to appreciate the significance of this event, it is necessary to understand some Dutch history. In the late eighteenth century, the evil influence of the French Enlightenment had infiltrated Dutch society and the Dutch church. Enlightenment ideas were forced upon the Dutch when Napoleon conquered the United Provinces and set up the Batavian Republic. Separation of church and state was instituted, but the state was not neutral; it had an antagonistic attitude to anything Christian.[9]

After the defeat of Napoleon, the House of Orange was restored, and a new constitution was issued by William I that gave religious freedom to all but declared that the state had a special concern for the Reformed church. Unfortunately, this paternalism more often resulted in state controls than in benefits for the Dutch church. The king gave the Reformed church a new church order that was hierarchical rather than Presbyterian in nature, one which gave the state authority to supervise various aspects of the work of synods.

Meanwhile, the spiritual renewal that had begun in the pietistic churches in Germany reached Holland, further dividing the state church between those who accepted a state-approved, dead formalism and those who embraced a thorough-going, evangelical Christianity. Eventually, a conflict arose between the two factions over the new forms of subscription to the church's doctrinal statement. Because the new form of subscription of 1816 was ambiguous and vague, some ministers claimed they could sign it in good conscience and yet not be truly Reformed. The doctrinal standards, they argued, allowed for much diversity within the Dutch church.

Many Dutch Calvinists were convinced that the Enlightenment had laid the church waste. Among those who spoke out against the spirit of the era was the poet Willem Bilderdyk. Bilderdyk contrasted the existing state of decline with the glories of Holland's Calvinistic heritage. In 1834, led by Y.P. Scholte, some of these Christians broke away from the state church in a movement called the Afscheiding (secession) and founded their own churches. Meanwhile, the ideas of the French Enlightenment continued to work towards the secularization of Dutch society as well as the Church.

Enter Guillaum Groen van Prinsterer. Although Groen did not join the Afscheiding, he shared many of its concerns and worked with conservatives in the state church to reform it. Groen was both a historian (archivist for the House of Orange-Nassau) and a statesman (he served in Parliament). But, his greatest achievement was to found Holland's Anti-Revolutionary party.

According to Groen, the spirit of the French Revolution was the greatest threat to Dutch society, indeed, to
all Christendom. This spirit, he argued, placed man
and his selfish desires above all consideration of God's
laws.

> The history of irreligious philosophy of the past
> century is in its source and its results, the teach-
> ing which, freely developed, destroys Church
> and State, society and family, produces disor-
> der without ever founding liberty or establish-
> ing moral order, and, in matters of religion,
> infallibly leads its conscientious followers to
> atheism and despair.[10]

Groen became an expert on revolution. "The defining feature of the Revolution," he asserted,

> is its hatred of the Gospel, its anti-Christian
> nature. This feature marks the Revolution, not
> when it "deviates from its course" and "lapses
> into excesses," but, on the contrary, precisely
> when it holds to its course and reaches the
> conclusion of its system, the true end of its
> logical development. This mark belongs to the
> Revolution. The Revolution can never shake it
> off. It is inherent in its very principle, and ex-
> presses and reflects its essence. It is the sign of
> its origin. It is the mark of hell.[11]

Groen was correct. As a historical movement, the
French Revolution, with all its horrors, had been the
logical result of years of humanistic thinking. France's
Christian population—the Huguenots—had been either
killed or harried out of France, thus destroying any
Christian witness. The vacuum was filled with atheistic
thinkers such as Voltaire and Rousseau, making France
the most radical country in Europe, hence the expression, "When France sneezes, the whole world catches
cold." Thus, the storming of the Bastille is not to be

associated with the "shot heard round the world" at Lexington in America. In America, the evils of war were restrained and kept in check by a Christian climate of opinion, an atmosphere that had been reinforced by the Great Awakening. In France, there was no such Christian influence, and the result was a reign of terror.

Radical leaders sought only their own advancement. Upon hearing a mob outside in the street, Robespierre told his servant: "Go downstairs and find out where they are going so that I may lead them." The Goddess of Reason was paraded through streets that flowed with innocent blood; the calendar, since it was based on the birth of Christ, was abolished and a new one developed that made the French Revolution, not the birth of Christ, the central movement in history. By 1772, the revolution had consumed most of its leaders (too late, unfortunately, for the French people) and had gone full circle back to autocracy—instead of the Sun King, the upstart Napoleon.[12]

Groen van Prinsterer understood all this and had seen the ill effects of the Enlightenment and the French Revolution in Holland. Convinced that all Christians must be "anti-revolutionary" in their political convictions, he founded Holland's Anti-Revolutionary party. (*Anti* should be taken in the sense of *instead of* and not as *counter*. The motto of the party was "Instead of Revolution, the Gospel."[13]) Yet, Groen was not reactionary. He argued that true sovereignty in society is derived from and resides in God alone—and not in the people, the state, or the monarch.

In order to bring everything into obedience to God, Groen championed the Word of God. His rallying cry: "It is written and it has happened." He believed that Christianity offered the only realistic answer to the problem of modern society, and that Reformed Christians needed to press their program without compromise on Dutch society. His commitment to Christian distinctiveness in politics became the watchword of the Anti-Revolutionary party: "In our isolation is our strength."[14] What he meant was this: while he desired rapprochement with other political parties, the Anti-Revolutionary party must remain independent and separate through loyalty to its own standpoint and principles, for therein lay its strength.

This, then, was the man whom Kuyper met in 1869. Groen's mantle would eventually fall to Kuyper, who would carry Groen's conservative Christian views into the next generation and into the highest elective office in the land.

On 6 March 1870, Dr. Kuyper accepted the call to minister in the Amsterdam state church. Although he had only been at Utrecht for three years, he was convinced the call was from the Lord. As the chief city of the Netherlands, Amsterdam was the perfect base from which to work towards the reformation of the Dutch church. Preaching in various sanctuaries belonging to the Amsterdam church, Kuyper became known as a great orator. Not only was Kuyper a master of the Dutch language, he also had a passion for the reformation of the Dutch church. His sermons were works of art. Even his reading of the Scriptures produced an indelible impression upon the minds of his hearers. As late as 1947, Dr. Grosheide remembered: "In a public meeting many years ago I heard Dr. Kuyper read the 148th Psalm. The impression which that reading made on me remains to this day. That distinctive, characteristic reading manner gave a better insight into the Psalm than four or five explanations would have done."[15] Dr. Kuyper's ability to speak would stand him in good stead later as a member of Parliament.

In 1870, the editor of *De Heraut* died unexpectedly, and Kuyper accepted the invitation to carry on the work. Dr. Kuyper then organized the Heraut Society, which bought the paper to insure that it would continue to disseminate the Reformed message. Its high goal was boldly printed on its masthead: "For a free church and a free school in a free land." Through this weekly, Kuyper immensely widened and deepened his influence. Too often, especially today, the power of the media is used for the de-Christianization of society. In this case, it was being used for good. About this same time, Dr. Kuyper used his influence to insure that the children in the municipal orphanage in Amsterdam would attend religious services conducted solely by orthodox pastors.

On 14 March 1871, Dr. Kuyper delivered (first in Amsterdam and later in some other cities in Holland) a lecture entitled *Modernism a Fata Morgana in the Realm of Christianity*. (The Fata Morgana is an unusual aerial phenomenon that takes place on occasion along the straits of Messina. For a short time, one sees high above the horizon, houses, places, towers, entire cities, all in constant motion and continuous change. Although entrancingly beautiful, it has no substance and only reflects what already exists.) According to Kuyper, liberal theology was little more than unreal forms and shadows, just like the Fata Morgana. A few excerpts give us the flavor of the work: "The god of the liberal theologians is an abstraction"; "As to their evolutionistic conception of man—if his moral nature evolved from something in the heart, there can be no talk of morality": "Nor do they possess a correct knowledge of sin. To their mind sin is an inner unrest, a never-slumbering remorse, a restless being driven by the moral ideal. But that moral ideal, too, is unreal."[16] The lecture later went out as a brochure, earning for Kuyper the gratitude of the conservatives and the wrath of the liberals.

In 1872, Kuyper heated up the battle by founding a daily newspaper, which would not only report the news but have a conservative Christian editorial view-

point. Called *De Standaard* (The Standard), the paper
was launched on 1 April 1872, the tercentenary of the
capture of Brielle by Dutch patriots from the hated
Spanish during the Dutch Revolt. The significance of
the date was not lost on Kuyper's friends or his enemies: *De Standaard* would be a banner around which
Christians could rally, a banner that stood for the
Reformed principles that guided in the founding of
the Dutch nation. The year also saw Kuyper organize
a new Anti-Revolutionary Voters Club in Amsterdam,
a prototype of the local clubs that would help organize
the party at the grassroots level. A man of extraordi-
nary vision, Kuyper was not concerned with instant
success or discouraged by failure. His eye was on the
future. About this time he wrote:

> We are working for the future. We are not con-
> cerned with the seeming victory of the moment
> but with the final triumph. With us the question
> is not what influence we can exert now but
> what power we can exercise 50 years hence, not
> how few men we have today, but how many will
> arise out of the younger generation who will be
> men of our principles. We know how to prac-
> tice patience. We know that the fruit cannot be
> plucked before the harvest time has arrived. Yet
> we also know that the hour of victory will some
> day come.[17]

Men with vision like Kuyper's are almost always
selfless, since such a hope means that the visionary
may not be around to enjoy the fruits of his labor.

So far, Dr. Kuyper had championed a full-orbed
Christianity in church affairs, journalism, and education. (Dr. Kuyper had long fought for equal rights
before the law for Christian schools with public schools.)
He had also written on politics and founded a local
political club. But, would Christian ideas work in the
real world of political intrigue and compromise, or

would Kuyper and his Christian followers be defense-
less sheep in a den of wolves?

Kuyper was persuaded that Christianity offered the
only hope for his nation. He was convinced that Holland needed Christian principles from the bottom of
society right on up to the top. He was well aware of the
fact that a society cannot be reformed from the top
down; hence, he never gave up his work in journalism,
in preaching, or in education. But, he also knew that
if a society was to be changed, such a change had to
involve the government as well. Accordingly, he stood
for office for the Gouda district for the first time in
1873. Although Kuyper lost the general election, he
gained valuable political experience that would later
help him attain the highest elective office in the land.

In November 1873, Kuyper delivered a lecture at
Utrecht in which he explained why political liberty
developed only in Protestant lands. Entitled *Calvinism,
the Origin and Guarantee of our Constitutional Liberties: A
Netherlands Reflection*, the lecture gave a panoramic view
of the progress of liberty in the Western world, which,
according to Kuyper, was fueled by Christianity's emphasis on liberty under the law. Kuyper began by stat-
ing that the countries which developed the greatest
freedom—Switzerland, Holland, England, the United
States, and other nations in northern Europe—were the
lands where Calvinism had had the greatest influence.
The U.S., the country which had the greatest freedom,
had been founded by Puritans. England's free institutions came as a result of the struggle between Indepen-
dents and the Crown. France just missed developing
free institutions and avoiding the French Revolution
by expelling the Huguenots, who took their talents and
their ideas on self-government to England and America.
Nations may live for a time off their Calvinistic inheritance, but eventually tyranny will result unless there is
a new influx of Christianity—a spiritual revival.[18]

Of the Bible's influence in creating the free society, John Chamberlain wrote in *The Roots of Capitalism*:

> One needs no paraphernalia of scholarship to know that the commandment against murder is simply the other face of Locke's and Jefferson's "unalienable" right to life. "Thou shalt not steal" means that the Bible countenances private property—for if a thing is not owned in the first place it can scarcely be stolen. "Thou shalt not covet" means that it is sinful even to contemplate the seizure of another man's goods—which is something which socialists, whether Christian or other, have never managed to explain away. Furthermore, the prohibition against false witness and adultery mean that contracts should be honored and double-dealing eschewed. As for the commandment to "honor thy father and thy mother that thy days may be long," this implies that the family, not the state, is the basic continuing unit and constitutive element of society.[19]

Although Chamberlain was thinking primarily of Great Britain and America, his words apply equally well to Holland. And, as Max Weber pointed out long ago, there seems to be a direct relationship between the Calvinist idea that every man has a calling—not just in religious profession, but in business as well—and the spirit of capitalism. According to Weber, Calvinism's emphasis on sobriety, thrift, upright conduct, and dedication to one's calling led, as a side effect, to capitalist accumulation and investment. In Holland, Calvinism's emphasis on thrift had its effects even on the rulers—the princes of Orange lived in a large house rather than a palace, had no entourage and chose to walk rather than ride in a carriage.

Calvinism also served to strengthen and nurture a deeper Western tradition, the idea of the dignity of each individual. Not only did all Western creeds be-

lieve that man is created in God's image, but Martin
Luther gave further impetus to the idea by emphasizing the "priesthood of the believer." When one accepts
the idea that every man has right both to read and
interpret the Scriptures for himself, it's just a short
intellectual journey to believing that every man has a
right to make economic and political decisions for
himself as well. Along with respect for the individual
came respect for property, for without property the
individual cannot be sustained.

Along with this emphasis on the dignity of man,
economic vitality was promoted by some of the lowest
interest rates in Europe. In the fifteenth century, interest rates fell from 14 percent to 5 percent; by the
sixteenth century, they were the lowest in Europe. In
England, where the interest rates were twice what they
were in Holland, the London merchant Josiah Child
saw how important they were in producing Holland's
economic miracle. "This in my poor opinion," wrote
Child, "is the causa causans of all the other causes of
riches in that people; and if interest of money were
with us reduced to the same rate as it is with them, it
would in a short time render us rich and considerable
in trade as they are."

Although governments can manipulate interest rates
through a central bank and by increasing or decreasing
their fiat currencies, such policies always cause serious
economic dislocations. True interest rates are a reflection of a country's basic philosophic and theological
outlook. If a given society is rife with anarchy, pessi-
mism, and rulers who try to regulate everything but
refuse to carry out their legitimate functions of protecting people from evildoers both within and without,
the price of money will be very high. People with money
will either send it out of the country or spend it immediately. It is this kind of "eat, drink, and be merry, for
tomorrow we die" philosophy that causes high interest
rates.[20]

On the other hand, if a society encourages thrift, self-government, hard work, and morality, and the government confines itself to its police functions, there are few risks in lending money. In such a society, people are more likely to forego present consumption, since the widespread stability tells them that there will be a future to be enjoyed.

This was the kind of attitude that prevailed in the early Dutch Republic, an attitude that came from Christianity, as expressed through Calvinism. Self-government under God—this was the key to freedom in the Western world. Dutch legal scholar Hugo Grotius put it this way:

> He knows not how to rule a Kingdom, that cannot manage a Province; nor can he wield a province, that cannot order a city; nor can he order a city, that knows not how to regulate a Village; nor he a village, that cannot guide a family; nor can that man govern well a family that knows not how to govern himself; neither can he govern himself unless his reason be Lord, will and appetite be vassals: nor can reason rule unless herself be ruled by God and (wholly) obedient to Him.[21]

These were some of the ideas which led to the development of freedom in Holland, indeed, in the Western world. Kuyper was determined to see these ideas renewed and revitalized.

On 21 January 1874, in an interim election, Kuyper was elected to the Second Chamber of Parliament by a vote of 1504 to 1252. Unfortunately, the Dutch Constitution stipulated in Article Ninety-one that clergymen could not serve in Parliament, so Kuyper reluctantly gave up his pulpit. Was it wrong for a minister of the Gospel to resign to serve in politics? In most cases, probably yes. Ultimately, a society can only be changed by the preaching of the Gospel; preaching is the most important activity.

Kuyper, however, was uniquely qualified to serve in the capacity as a Christian magistrate. Men like Groen van Prinsterer were excellent speakers and writers. Yet, they themselves did not have the ability, as Kuyper did, to bring the Christian political message down to the voter. Moreover, through his work in the Church, Kuyper was helping to train a generation of ministers who could preach the Gospel throughout Holland. Kuyper, then, appeared to be God's man for the hour. Just as God calls certain men to be Christian carpenters or Christian medical doctors, so he calls certain men to labor in the field of politics. Kuyper felt that he was such a man. If Jesus sought out tax collectors, Kuyper would seek out those who wrote the tax codes.

When Kuyper entered Parliament, there were four major parties in Holland: the Liberals, who were trying to translate Enlightenment ideas into Dutch political life; the Conservatives, who had essentially the same presuppositions as the Liberals but wanted change to occur gradually; the Catholics, who had recently broken with the Liberals over the latter's endorsement of secularized education in the public schools; and the Anti-Revolutionaries, who were for the most part a Christian Reformed party. On occasion, the Anti-Revolutionaries would combine with the Catholics and Conservatives against the Liberals, who had the greatest influence of any party.[22]

When Kuyper went to the Hague, the government was headed by a Liberal faction, the DeVries cabinet; a few months later, the Heemskerk ministry was formed, resulting in a coalition government of Liberals and the other groups. The first issue that Kuyper faced as a young congressman (he was thirty-six—the second youngest) concerned the nation's schools. In the name of modernizing education, the government wanted to strip education of any Christian elements. At the same time, it wanted to put new demands on the private schools, making it more difficult for them to stay in existence. To these proposals, Kuyper answered a resounding "no." Kuyper, championing parental rights, advocated less government control over education. If the government insisted on certain burdensome requirements, the government should finance them and they should be administered locally by private school officials. In late nineteenth century Holland, a school system completely free of government control such as in early America was unknown. In suggesting government aid for private schools, Kuyper was working within the constraints of his society. Because of the opposition from Kuyper and other Anti-Revolutionaries, the bill died.

A second major problem that Parliament faced was the colonial question. How should Holland treat the restless millions who lived under her rule in the Dutch East Indies? Kuyper pushed for the Christianization of the Indies and the end of the opium trade. Unfortunately, these reforms were never promoted as aggressively as Kuyper would have liked. Finally, Kuyper advocated the codification and clarification of laws protecting the workingman in order to check the specter of Communism, which was raising its ugly head in Europe.

In order to take a break from his work and gain spiritual refreshment, Kuyper traveled across the English Channel to Brighton to attend a series of revival meetings led by the American evangelist Dwight L. Moody. Kuyper was blessed by the meetings and returned to Holland writing and speaking about the evangelical revival that he hoped would spread to the Dutch church. Unfortunately, Kuyper's many labors—editing a daily newspaper, working in Parliament, and preaching and lecturing on Sundays—became too much for him, and he suffered a complete breakdown. Things were so bad that he could not read more than two pages in one sitting or write so much as one postcard. Exhausted, Kuyper was sent by his doctors to southern Europe, Italy, and Switzerland, where he regained his strength and developed a life-long interest in mountain-climbing. After fifteen months, he felt he could return home.

The Abraham Kuyper who returned to Holland in 1877 was a new man with a new strategy. Up to this point, he had been a "one-man show." His efforts had been almost superhuman. But, Kuyper was a man, and he could not reform Holland all by himself. His nervous breakdown and enforced exile had taught him that. So, from 1877 to 1880, Kuyper dedicated himself to going back and building a stronger foundation, one upon which a Christian society could be built. Such activities included publishing a weekly religious paper once again; turning the Anti-Revolutionary party into a full-fledged national party complete with local, regional, and national offices; and founding a new university—the Free University of Amsterdam.

The founding of the Free University of Amsterdam was one of the greatest achievements of Kuyper's life. In 1877, Holland had three universities—those at Leiden, Groningen, and Utrecht. All three were state schools. As went the state, so went the universities. Unfortunately, the Modernists had been in control of the government and the universities, making the schools little more than seminaries of secular humanism. In order to train a generation of leaders to counteract this influence, Kuyper founded the Free University. As one might expect, it was no easy task. After one year of fundraising, promotion, hiring, and prayer, the Free University opened its doors on 20 October 1880.

In using the word *Free* as part of the university's name, Dr. Kuyper was drawing attention to his philoso-

phy of sphere sovereignty. According to this philosophy, each institution in society has its God-given rights
and should be free to fulfill its purpose under God.
The main purpose of the church, for example, is to
preach the Gospel. It should be sovereign in that area.
The main purpose of the government is to protect life
and property. It too, should be free to pursue its mandate. Schools should be free to carry out their mission
of education—free of government control. Occasion-
ally, responsibilities overlap, but, essentially, all institutions should police themselves, and all are ultimately
responsible to God. The Free University, then, was
designed to be free of government control as well as of
church control. (The fact that the church was domi-
nated by liberals showed that church control was no
guarantee of orthodoxy.) To Americans, a free university does not seem so strange, for America's most pres-
tigious universities, such as Harvard and Princeton, are
still private; but, for the Dutch, this was something
quite new.

For years, the Free University turned out hundreds
of Christian theologians, doctors, lawyers, and preachers—leaders who helped inform Dutch society with
Christian principles. And, Dr. Kuyper, of course, was
for many years one of the chief professors, teaching at
one time or another, in almost every department. He
was a true Renaissance Man, a man who could do
everything well. Or, better yet, he was a true Reformation Man—a man who attempted to use all of his talents
for the Lord.[23]

In 1883, the State Church of Holland took another
step towards apostasy when the doctrinal standards for
ministers-to-be were watered down even more than in
the past. Kuyper saw the writing on the wall; there was
no other course of action but to withdraw from the
state church. By 1887, some two hundred congregations, with a total membership of one hundred thou-

sand, had left the state church under Kuyper's leadership. The result was the Christian Reformed church. The formation of this new denomination was not without its birth pangs, however. The state church tried to destroy it in its infancy by seizing, using state police forces, all the property of the congregations that had withdrawn from the state church. Tension increased so much that there were threats against Kuyper's life. The local police offered him a bodyguard of plainclothes officers, but he declined the offer. "I place my life in the hand of God," he told them. For the rest of his life, Kuyper championed the rights of this new church.[24]

Throughout the 1880s, although Kuyper held no national political office, he was the acknowledged leader of the Anti-Revolutionary party. He served as chairman at meetings of the National Committee; presiding officer and keynote speaker at the national conventions; editor of *De Standaard*; campaign manager and speaker; and as a political observer, all the while keeping his hand on the operation of all levels of party organization.

In 1887, Kuyper made a decisive move—one that showed he realized the need to cooperate with other political groups when they found themselves on the same side of an issue. When the Anti-Revolutionary party met in convention, they received overtures from the Roman Catholics. Although Kuyper could never worship with the Catholics, he could work with them to protect private schools. After all, a Roman Catholic was as much a Dutch citizen as was a member of the Christian Reformed church. Without such cooperation, neither the Catholics nor Kuyper's party would have much legislative success; the Liberals would have continued to dominate Parliament. Such cooperation should not be equated with modern movements to bring Protestantism and Catholicism together, however. Kuyper understood that the two could never walk to-

gether unless they were in agreement—and Catholics
and Reformed people would never agree on all points.
Kuyper had pointed this out in 1872, when he published a reprint brochure on the St. Bartholomew's
Day Massacre. He also pointed out the errors of Roman Catholicism in his articles in De Heraut. One
might say that although Kuyper could not worship with
Roman Catholics, he could work with them as fellow
Dutch citizens.[25]

As a politician, Kuyper realized the importance of
detail work and grassroots organization as much as
giving a major policy speech at a national convention.

In 1891, Kuyper gave a speech at the Anti-Revolutionary party convention that expressed his belief that
there were essentially only two competing worldviews—
the Christian and the anti-Christian. The Anti-Revolutionaries, he declared, follow the Bible, while all the
other parties hail the worship of man. His conclusion:
the party must

> cling to the banner of the Cross, to go hero-
> ically into battle, not for personal honor or
> power, for high office or financial gain, but for
> the Christ and His future, and in connection
> with that future of our Lord, for the spiritual
> deliverance of our country, so that, when Christ
> returns, there will be found on our soil, too,
> which once received the blood of the martyrs,
> a people that does not strive against Him, but
> hails Him with a Hallelujah!

In the party platform that year, Kuyper pressed for
a reform that he had long advocated: head of house-
hold voting. The 1800s and the early 1900s were the
great age of expanding the franchise in Western Europe and America. But, Kuyper didn't jump on the
bandwagon and push for universal suffrage. The family, said Kuyper, was the basis of society. Therefore,
heads of households should be the ones to vote. Usually on the conservative side of political issues, since

Holland had a Christian heritage worth preserving, he
was now progressive in that he wanted to expand the
franchise, but with limitations. Depending on the time
and culture, a Christian statesman can be either progressive or conservative; progressive if it means mov-
ing away from the tired ideas of humanism towards
Christianity; conservative, if it means conserving a
Christian patrimony. The Christian is, moreover, a true
liberal in the nineteenth century's sense of the word:
he believes in liberty under God.

But, politics is a practical business, and Kuyper was
forced merely to support a bill which extended the
franchise in general. In Kuyper's view, allowing the
sturdy Dutch artisans and farmers to vote along with
the upper classes posed no threat to Dutch society.

Frank Vandenberg, Kuyper's chief biographer in
English, put it this way:

> Kuyper's politics were not some accidental, op-
> portunistic assortment of ideas on the questions
> of the day, but the product of his life philoso-
> phy. The chief, all-governing principle of
> Kuyper's political science can be set down briefly
> thus: to declare in the political area, too, not
> only by the word of profession but also by deeds
> of legislation and administration, the absolute
> sovereignty of God and the supreme validity of
> divine ordinances for the life of the people and
> the nation.[26]

In 1901, Kuyper and the Right drove the forces of
liberalism and socialism out of the majority in Parliament. As leader of the largest party in the Rightist
coalition, Kuyper was asked by Queen Wilhelmina to
form a cabinet. For years, Kuyper had written, published, taught, lectured, and organized. Now, he was
Prime Minister of one of the world's leading nations.
Could the Christian principles he had espoused really
work, or were Christians so heavenly-minded that they
could do no earthly good?

Kuyper would have said that the problem is that
Christians weren't heavenly-minded enough; the truly
practical man is the one who lives according to God's
standards. When we build an airplane, we don't build
it according to some pet theory, but according to the
laws that God has laid down in nature. By the same
token, when we build a society, we need to build it
according to the dictates of Scripture.

In order to fulfill the Queen's mandate, Kuyper
took a leave of absence from the Free University and
moved to The Hague. He was sixty-four years old. To
understand Kuyper's role as a Prime Minister, let us
consider the five major issues that confronted the
Kuyper government.

First, there was Queen Wilhelmina's sickness.
Shortly after Kuyper took office, the queen fell sick.
For a time, it looked as if she would die. And, since the
queen must sign all legislation, a major constitutional
crisis was in the making. Providentially, God spared
the life of this queen, thus saving Holland as well as
Kuyper from much difficulty. The whole legislative
process, however, had been at a standstill during her
illness. Throughout the crisis, the Prime Minister was
a tower of strength and quiet faith in God. Kuyper
inspired confidence, not alarm.

The next major issue that confronted Kuyper was
the Boer War. The Boers were the descendants of
Dutch farmers who had settled in South Africa, and
they still had strong ties to Holland. Now, the British
Empire was about to absorb them just as she had so
many other peoples before. And, the Boer War was no
ordinary war. The British abandoned their "civilized"
way of fighting and committed numerous atrocities.
Some of the world's first concentration camps were set
up to hold Boer women and children so that they
could not offer aid and comfort to Boer guerrilla fight-
ers. Thousands were dying, and the Boer republics in
South Africa appealed to Holland for help.[27]

Kuyper did not want to go to war against England. Holland was no longer a match for the great British Empire. But, he could not just sit back and let fellow Dutchmen, many of them Christians, be wiped out by England. Kuyper's response was to continually lobby the British government to make peace in South Africa. Eventually, Kuyper prevailed, but not until great damage had been done, the consequences of which we are still feeling today.

The greatest domestic crisis of Kuyper's administration came when a small but important group of railroad workers went on strike. Instigated by the radical socialist element that was beginning to raise its ugly head in many European countries, and supported by the socialists in Parliament, these strikes brought the whole of northern Europe's rail lines to a halt because of their strategic location, at the gateway to Germany. Soon, other rabble-rousers joined in, including Amsterdam's municipal workers, who tried to stop the operation of that city's entire water supply system. The shadow of anarchism began to fall across the land.

Kuyper was not about to let a small group of workers paralyze Holland's entire rail system, so on 24 February 1903, he introduced three bills in Parliament. The first set up a government railroad brigade which could be used to fill any gap that striking workers had created. The second bill called for the establishment of a government commission to investigate working conditions among the railroad workers. Finally, Kuyper proposed an anti-railroad strike law. If this bill became law, those who abandoned their posts, thereby endangering public safety, would be treated as criminals.

Kuyper's bills were opposed in Parliament by the Social Democrats, the Free Socialists, and the Anarchists. Kuyper was told that such harsh measures would incite even more riots. But, Kuyper knew the Dutch people too well; despite humanism's inroads, there was a strong enough Christian influence to support Kuyper's proposals. Kuyper's bills passed by large margins. Radical leaders called for a general strike, but rescinded the call when they saw that Kuyper would not back down. Two thousand railroad workers were fired, along with four hundred Amsterdam city workers. These events caused many Christians to realize that they needed to form their own unions, since the secular ones had been infiltrated by Marxists and were anti-Christian.

Kuyper's legislation was an unqualified success: since 1903, there has never been a railroad strike in Holland, and the laws are still on the statute books.[28] Had Kuyper not worked with the citizenry that had a Christian heritage and respected the rule of law, the outcome would have been quite different. When revolutionaries called for strikes in Russia at about the same time, there was not a sufficient Christian base (Russia had had no Reformation) to restrain the mob.

The fourth major problem during Kuyper's administration was the issue of higher education. In order to promote his ideas on higher education as well as the welfare of the Netherlands, Kuyper carefully guided the Higher Education Law of 1905 through Parliament. The law had several important provisions. First, it put final exams at non-public universities on a par with exams at public universities. Previously, students going to the Free University, a private school, had to take two sets of final exams: their own at the Free University, and another set at a state university to have their diplomas validated. Under this system, teachers at the Free University were forced to "teach to the test" and teach certain secular orthodoxies as being true. Such practices take away from true education. Kuyper's bill changed all that by granting effectus civilis to non-public university diplomas. The bill also stipulated that private citizens and church groups could found university chairs at the state universities, thus allowing for a diversity of opinions even in state-controlled schools. Finally, the bill opened up the way for the founding of technological universities to help Holland remain competitive in the twentieth century. (The first of these would be the Delft Polytechnic School.)

Kuyper's bill passed the Second Chamber of Parliament, but not the First. But, because Kuyper didn't feel the First Chamber accurately represented the political will of Holland (not to mention the fact that it didn't support his bill), he dissolved the Chamber with the permission of the queen. New elections were held. With the Right—and Kuyper's allies—now in the majority, Kuyper's bill passed. Kuyper was accused by the Liberals of using high-handed tactics, but he had done everything legally and according to parliamentary procedure.

Success often breeds complacency, or a false sense of security. Thus, when the 1905 elections approached, there was dissension on the Right. But, the Christian conservatives had not yet consolidated their power, and didn't have the luxury to be able to disagree. Meanwhile, while Kuyper was running the government, the Liberals were working day and night to defeat him. The 1905 election was one of the great disappointments of his life, as the Rightist coalition went down to defeat. On 16 August, the Kuyper cabinet retired. Holland would never experience such outstanding Christian leadership again.

Kuyper's government hadn't passed many laws. The Liberals often criticized his government on this point. But, if anything, a multitude of laws is indicative of a sick society. When a people is self-governing, there is little need for a torrent of laws. On the other hand, when people no longer govern themselves, the civil government tends to fill a vacuum and seeks to regulate every aspect of life. Eventually, such a profusion of laws does more damage than it does good. As one

American congressman said, "Whenever Congress adjourns and I come home, my father says, 'Thank God—the country is safe again.' " Kuyper's government may not have passed many laws, but it did much to fulfill the mandate of Romans 13. In addition, Kuyper's government was responsible for beginning the practice of appointing mayors whose political affiliation coincided with the political make-up of the towns they served and in getting a liquor law passed that limited the sale of liquor—much to the benefit of Dutch society.

Kuyper chose not to run for Parliament after he lost the Prime Minister's job. His plan: let the DeMuster government show how weak the Liberals are. The people will then turn to the Christians for answers and the Right will be swept into power and be able to enact their agenda for Holland.

In 1907, Kuyper took over the leadership of the party from Dr. Herman Bavinck. In 1908, he was elected to fill a vacancy for the Ommen district in Gelderland, but by 1912 he was forced to resign because of hearing and health problems. Nevertheless, he continued to be a prolific writer. In the 1913 campaign alone, he wrote more than two hundred articles espousing the Anti-Revolutionary cause.

In 1914, the lights went out all across Europe, with the beginning of World War I. As an elder statesman and a national leader, Kuyper was forced to declare for one side or the other. He chose Germany. It was the logical choice for a Dutchman in the early twentieth century. This was not the Germany of Adolf Hitler—it was a kingdom and no more responsible for the war than France or Russia. Moreover, the Dutch and Germans are very closely related. Dutch citizens living on the border with Germany can read a German newspaper, while Germans traveling through Holland can understand most of the traffic signs, printed in Dutch. In the nineteenth century, some Germans predicted that Holland would be part of a Greater Germany—a Gross Deutschland. So, it is not difficult to understand why Kuyper sided with Germany. (At the end of the war, when Kaiser Wilhelm abdicated, he fled to friendly Holland.) Of course, Kuyper would never have sided with Hitler and his Nazi thugs. Indeed, it was Kuyper's followers with their Christian principles who opposed Nazism both in Germany and in Holland.[29]

Kuyper's last years were spent watching younger men take over the leadership of organizations he had created or fostered in their infancy. It was a humbling experience for this man who had been a leader since he was a child. Step by step, God loosened his grip on the party leadership, the editorship of the newspaper, his teaching position, and other responsibilities. Finally, at about six o'clock in the evening on 8 November 1920, Kuyper passed away. Tributes poured in from all over Holland and the world, while the Prime Minister gave a memorial address in parliament. There were thousands of mourners at the funeral, but not a single flower. That had been his request. Kuyper would rather see the money ordinarily spent on flowers go towards causes in which he believed.

How important was he to history? "Eliminate Kuyper," wrote Vandenberg, "and you cannot understand Dutch history of about the last 80 years." Kuyper is gone, his life a part of Dutch history. But, his life purpose can still live on in the lives of present-day Christians. "In the total expanse of human life there is not a single square inch of which the Christ, who alone is sovereign does not declare, 'That is mine.' " May we, like Kuyper, continue to claim souls and the world for Him.

Chapter Ten

Conclusion

As we have seen in the preceding pages, not only is it legitimate for Christians to be involved in politics; they have been, for centuries. They have served as kings, prime ministers, lawmakers, and governors in the world's leading nations. In many cases, they were the decisive forces in shaping their societies' climates of opinion. John Witherspoon was the virtual "Grandfather of the U.S. Constitution." William Wilberforce abolished slavery in the British Empire and set the Christian tone of Victorian England. William Bradford and John Winthrop founded what is now the world's only superpower. In fact, nearly all the free institutions that we enjoy are the outgrowth of biblical principles applied to politics.

Today, men like Witherspoon, Wilberforce, Bradford, and Winthrop are gone. We need new men and women to stand in the gap and become involved in the great moral battles of today. With the United States government now consuming as large a percentage of its GNP as Communist China does of its GNP, and with the average taxpayer paying nearly 50 percent of his income in taxes, Christians cannot avoid becoming involved in politics. What were once—and still should be—personal and private decisions are now political issues. And, until we drastically limit the size and scope of government, it will continue to usurp the rightful role of the church, the family, the private sector, and the individual.

This doesn't mean, however, that Christians need to give up their other Christian duties and become full-time politicians. True, some Christians will be called into politics, as was Abraham Kuyper. But, if every Christian would vote consistently, in primaries as well as in general elections, and take on just one more responsibility, whether it's as a dog-catcher or county committee person, we would be well on our way to restoring the American Republic. The problem is that many Christians don't even vote on a regular basis. They get excited about a candidate, elect a Ronald Reagan as president, then go home for the next decade, only to wake up and find Bill Clinton in the White House. To see real positive changes, Christians need to approach their responsibilities as citizens as they should all their other responsibilities—with balance, and daily and weekly consistency. Such a life, lived out over sixty or seventy years, can make a real difference.

But, while working to limit government and return it to its proper Biblical functions—protecting property and life (including the lives of the unborn)—we need to work at restoring society's other God-given institutions. Until the church is restored to its former greatness—preaching the Gospel, and witnessing against evil—we can't expect to elect godly people to government. Most important of all is the family, which is everyone's first church, first government, and first school. Until the family is restored and government taken out of the business of usurping the family, we can't expect to produce the stable, self-governing individuals necessary to maintain a republic.

At the end of the twentieth century, we find ourselves in the same situation as Nehemiah in the fifth century B.C. Seeking to rebuild the walls of Jerusalem and his broken society, he had to be ever-vigilant, working with a trowel in one hand and a sword in the other. I'm sure that most Christians would like to give their full attention to either building or fighting—not both. Nehemiah would have liked to have had the same luxury. Yet, that is what God called both him and us to do in our respective ages.

If you are a Christian, the time has come to live a consistent Christian daily walk, applying the Bible to all aspects of life—family, education, business, ministry, and yes, government. God has called us to engage the world, to be in it, but not of it. Ultimately, what we really need, as John Witherspoon reminded us, is spiritual revival: "We have no warrant to ask for national prosperity," he told his congregation in Scotland, "without a revival of religion."

One of the clearest calls to revival was given in 1801, by Timothy Dwight, another Christian statesman who served both as president of Yale and as a delegate to the Massachusetts State House. To his students he said:

> To this end you must coolly, firmly, and irrevocably make your determination, and resolve, that Jehovah is your God, and that you will serve Him only.... Let me at the same time warn you, that your enemies are numerous, industrious, and daring, full of subtlety, and full of zeal.... In this contest you may be left alone. Fear not; they that be for you will even then be more than they that are against you. Almighty Power will protect, Infinite Wisdom will guide, and Unchangeable Goodness will prosper you. The Christian world rises daily in prayer to heaven for your faithfulness and success; the host of sleeping saints calls to you from the grave, and bids you Godspeed. The spirits of your fathers lean from yonder skies to survey

the conflict, and your children of many generations, will rise up, and call you blessed.

The result was the Second Great Awakening, which
reinforced the Christian principles upon which America
was founded, led to the formation of the American
Tract, Bible, and Home Missionary Societies, and the
effective preaching of Asahel Nettleton and Nathaniel
Taylor. The founding of America's foreign mission
movement also dates from this period. Had one more
revival occurred at mid-century, slavery might have been
phased out legally—as was done in the British Empire—
and the Civil War averted. (Sufficient credit has never
been given by most historians to those Christian statesmen who worked to avert civil war and do away with
slavery peacefully.)

The world today is in need of Christians like the
men in this book, who served God, their families, and
their countries (in that order). Under the influence of
such men and women, perhaps God will be pleased to
grant us yet another spiritual awakening.

Notes

Chapter One

1. Hugh Latimer, quoted in Antonia Fraser, ed., *The Lives of the Kings and Queens of England* (New York: Alfred A. Knopf, 1975), 189.

2. Richard Cox, quoted in Ibid., 190.

3. Ibid., 194.

4. John Calvin, quoted in W. Stanford Reid, ed., *John Calvin: His Influence in the Western World* (Grand Rapids: Zondervan Pub., 1982), 188.

5. David Harris Wilson and Stuart E. Prall, *A History of England* (1967; reprint, New York: Holt, Rinehart, and Winston, 1984), 106–107.

6. Martin Bucer to Calvin, quoted in Reid, *John Calvin*, 182.

7. Francis Bourgoyne to Calvin, quoted in Ibid.

8. Ibid.

9. Calvin, quoted in Ibid., 183.

10. Ibid.

11. Ibid.

12. Calvin, quoted in Ibid., 187.

13. Calvin, quoted in Ibid., 186.

14. Ian H. Murray, *The Puritan Hope* (Edinburgh: The Banner of Truth Trust, 1971), 6.

15. Benjamin Hart, *Faith and Freedom* (San Bernardino, Calif.: Here's Life Publishers, Inc., 1988), 60.

16. King Edward VI, quoted in "The Reformation Conflict, Part II," *The Banner of Truth*, vol. 13, no. 2, 110.

Chapter Two

1. Cotton Mather, *Magnalia Christi Americana* (1702; reprint, Edinburgh: Banner of Truth, 1979), 110.

2. Bradford Smith, *Bradford of Plymouth* (Philadelphia: J.B. Lippincott Co., 1950).

3. Ibid., 51.

4. Mather, *Magnalia*, 110.

5. Mary B. Sherwood, *Pilgrim: A Biography of William Brewster* (Falls Church, Virginia: Great Oak Press of Virginia, 1982).

6. Smith, *Bradford*, 63.

7. William Bradford, *Of Plymouth Plantation*, ed. Samuel Eliot Morison (1952; reprint, New York: Alfred A. Knopf, 1982), 19–20.

8. Benjamin Hart, *Faith and Freedom* (San Bernardino, Calif.: Here's Life Publishers, Inc., 1988), 60.

9. Smith, *Bradford*, 78.

10. Bradford, *Of Plymouth Plantation*, 47.

11. Ibid., 75–76.

12. Jacques Choron, *Suicide* (New York: Charles Scribner's Sons, 1972), 25.

13. Smith, Bradford, 156.

14. Ibid., 166.

15. Bradford, *Of Plymouth Plantation*, 97.

16. Ibid., 120–121.

17. Ibid.

18. Smith, *Bradford*, 201.

19. Ibid., 202–203.

20. Ibid., 222.

21. Ibid., 228.

22. Ibid., 239.

23. Ibid., 253.

Chapter Three

1. Edmund S. Morgan, *The Puritan Dilemma: The Story of John Winthrop* (Boston: Little, Brown, and Co., 1958), 1–5.

2. Ibid., 6.

3. Ibid.

4. Ibid.

5. Ibid., 9.

6. Ibid., 11.

7. Ibid.

8. Ibid., 11–40.

9. Ibid., 41.

10. Ibid., 42.

11. Ibid., 49.

12. Ibid., 53.

13. John Winthrop, "A Model of Christian Charity," *The Puritans: A Sourcebook of Their Writings,* ed. by Perry Miller and Thomas H. Johnson (1938; reprint, New York: Harper and Row, 1963): 195–199.

14. Morgan, *The Puritan Dilemma,* 54.

15. Samuel Eliot Morison, *Builders of the Bay Colony* (1930; reprint, Boston: Houghton, Miflin, and Co., 1958), 82.

16. Ibid., 86.

17. Ibid., 84, 94.

18. Morgan, *The Puritan Dilemma,* 92.

19. Morison, *Builders,* 86.

20. Morgan, *The Puritan Dilemma,* 96.

21. Morison, *Builders,* 84.

22. Morgan, *The Puritan Dilemma,* 86.

23. Morison, *Builders,* 87.

24. Ibid., 90.

25. Morgan, *The Puritan Dilemma,* 115–133.

26. Ibid., 129.

27. Ibid., 131.

28. Ibid., 144.

29. Ibid., 151.

30. Ibid., 196.

31. Ibid.

32. Morison, *Builders,* 92.

33. Edmund S. Morgan, *The Puritan Family* (1944; reprint, New York: Harper and Row, 1966), 143.

34. Morgan, *The Puritan Family,* 97.

Chapter Four

1. Samuel Eliot Morison, *Builders of the Bay Colony* (Boston: Houghton Mifflin Co., 1930), 219.

2. Ibid., 221.

3. Ibid., 222.

4. Ibid., 222–223.

5. Ibid., 224.

6. Roderick Nash, *Wilderness and the American Mind* (n.p., n.d.)

7. Morison, *Builders*, 226.

8. Ibid., 230.

9. Ibid.

10. Morison, *Builders*, 231–232.

11. Perry Miller and Thomas H. Johnson, *The Puritans: A Sourcebook of Their Writings* (1938; reprint, New York: Harper and Row, 1963), 236.

12. Morison, *Builders*, 231.

13. Ibid., 232–234.

14. Miller and Johnson, *The Puritans*, 226–236.

15. Ibid., 227–228.

16. Robert A. Peterson, "Lessons in Liberty: The Dutch Republic, 1579-1750," *The Freeman*, vol. 37, no. 7 (July 1987): 261.

17. Roland Bainton, *The Travail of Religious Liberty* (Philadelphia: The Westminster Press, 1961), 22–23.

18. Miller and Johnson, *The Puritans*, 226.

Chapter Five

1. John Witherspoon, quoted in Charles Augustus Briggs, *American Presbyterianism* (New York: Charles Scribner's Sons, 1885), 351.

2. Varnum Lansing Collins, *President Witherspoon: A Biography* (Princeton: Princeton University Press, 1925), vol. 1, 14–18.

3. J. Dickie, "John Witherspoon, Patriot," n.d., MS, Presbyterian Historical Society Archives, Philadelphia, Pa., 9–10.

4. Ibid., 6.

5. Lyman H. Butterfield, *John Witherspoon Comes to America* (Princeton: Princeton University Library, 1953).

6. John Witherspoon, *The Works of John Witherspoon* (Edinburgh, Scotland: 1804–1805), vol. 2, 202–203.

7. Ibid.

8. Martha Lou Lennon Stohlman, *John Witherspoon* (Philadelphia: The Westminster Press, 1976), 120.

9. Ibid.

10. Ibid., 121.

11. Ibid., 122.

12. Ibid., 125.

13. Ibid., 127.

14. Ibid.

15. Ibid., 132.

16. Witherspoon, *Works*, vol. 4., 223.

17. John Witherspoon, *An Annotated Edition of Lectures on Moral Philosophy*, ed. Jack Scott (Newark: University of Delaware Press, 1982), 147.

18. Witherspoon, *Lectures on Moral Philosophy*, 168.

19. Ibid., 178.

20. Ibid., 218.

21. James H. Smylie, "Madison and Witherspoon: Theological Roots of American Political Thought," *The Princeton University Library Chronicle*, vol. XXII, no. 3 (Spring 1967): 121.

22. Witherspoon, "Part of a Speech for Congress, upon the Confederation," *Works* (Philadelphia, 1802), vol. 4, 350.

23. Witherspoon, *Lectures on Moral Philosophy*, 144. Italics mine.

24. Ibid.

25. Madison, *The Federalist*, no. 51, II (New York 1788): 118.

26. Witherspoon, *Lectures on Moral Philosophy*, 124.

27. Ibid.

28. Ibid., 126, 127.

29. Robert A. Peterson, "Lessons in Liberty: The Dutch Republic, 1579-1750" *The Freeman*, vol. 37, no. 7 (July 1987): 261.

30. Witherspoon, *Lectures on Moral Philosophy*, 144.

31. Ibid., 160.

32. Smylie, "Madison and Witherspoon," 130.

33. M.E. Bradford, *A Worthy Company* (Marlborough, N.H.: Plymouth Rock Foundation, 1982).

34. George Washington, *Farewell Address*, 1796.

35. Ralph Ketcham, *James Madison* (New York: Macmillan Co., 1971), 46.

36. Smylie, "Madison and Witherspoon," 131.

37. Richard Hofstadter, *The American Political Tradition* (New York: Vintage Books, 1948), 3.

38. Harold O.J. Brown, *The Reconstruction of the American Republic* (Milford, Mich.: Mott Media, 1981), 25.

39. Charles G. Osgood, *Lights in Nassau Hall* (Princeton: Princeton University Press, 1951), 12-13.

Chapter Six

1. John Munroe, *Federalist Delaware 1775-1815* (New Brunswick, N.J.: Rutgers University Press, 1954), 81.

2. M.E. Bradford, *A Worthy Company: Brief Lives of the Framers of the United States Constitution* (Marlborough, N.H.: Plymouth Rock Foundation, Inc., 1982), 110.

3. Robert E. Pattison, "The Life and Character of Richard Bassett," *Papers of the Historical Society of Delaware*, XXIX (Wilmington, The Historical Society of Delaware, 1900), 8, 9.

4. Munroe, *Federalist Delaware*, 81.

5. Ibid., 15.

6. Ibid., 88.

7. Carol E. Hoffecker, *Delaware: A Bicentennial History* (New York: W.W. Norton and Company, Inc., 1977), 88.

8. Francis Asbury, *The Journal and Letters of Francis Asbury*, edited by Elmer T. Clark, et. al. (Nashville: Abingdon Press, 1958), 1:263, 1:263-264, 1:398.

9. Munroe, *Federalist Delaware*, 240.

10. Nathaniel Luff, *Journal of the Life of Luff, M.D., of the State of Delaware* (New York, 1848), 61, 127.

11. Pattison, "The Life and Character," 13.

12. Ibid.

13. Ibid.

14. Hoffecker, *Delaware*, 89.

15. Pattison, "The Life and Character," 14.

16. Munroe, *Federalist Delaware*, 96.

17. Ibid., 142.

18. Ibid., 141.

19. Robert G. Ferris and James H. Charleton, *The Signers of the Constitution* (Arlington, Va.: Interpretive Publications, 1986), 142.

20. Munroe, *Federalist Delaware*, 107.

21. Ibid., 161.

22. Ibid., 158.

23. Bradford, *A Worthy Company*, 110.

24. Munroe, *Federalist Delaware*, 159.

25. Ibid., 163.

26. Ibid., 154.

27. Ibid., 154.

28. Bradford, *A Worthy Company*, 100.

29. Pattison, "The Life and Character," 19.

30. Robert Peterson, "A Tale of Two Revolutions," *The Freeman* (August 1989).

31. Munroe, *Federalist Delaware*, 152.

32. Pattison, "The Life and Character," 14.

33. John C. Miller, *The Federalist Era* (New York: Harper and Row Publishers, Harper Torch Books, 1960), 277.

34. Pattison, "The Life and Character," 19.

35. Ibid.

Chapter Seven

1. John Pollock, *Wilberforce* (Herts, England: Lion Publishing, 1977), 12.

2. Pollock, *Wilberforce*, 27.

3. Pollock, *Wilberforce*, 31.

4. Ibid., 24.

5. Ibid., 31–39.

6. Ibid., 38.

7. Charles Colson, *Kingdoms in Conflict* (Grand Rapids, Mich.: Zondervan Corp. and William Morrow, 1987), 99.

8. Pollock, *Wilberforce*, 43.

9. Ibid., 46, 67, 66.

10. Ibid., 61.

11. Ibid., 223, 165, 152, 184.

12. Ibid., 56.

13. Colson, *Kingdoms*, 100.

14. Ibid., 102.

15. Ibid., 103.

16. William Cowper, "The Negro's Complaint," *The Poems of William Cowper* (New York: Edward Kearny, N.D.), 365–366.

17. Herbert Welch, ed., *Selections from the Writings of Rev. John Wesley* (New York: Eaton and Mains, 1901), 336.

18. Pollock, *Wilberforce*, 194.

19. Ibid., 211–212.

20. Ibid., 171, 255.

21. Ibid., 234–235.

22. Ibid., 235.

23. Ibid., 23.

24. Richard Grenier, *The Gandhi Nobody Knows* (Nashville: Thomas Nelson Publishers, 1983), 118.

25. Pollock, *Wilberforce*, 237.

26. Ibid., 238.

27. Ibid., 223.

28. Ibid., 186.

29. Pollock mentions this in his biography.

30. Peter Gay and R.K. Webb, *Modern Europe Since 1815* (New York: Harper and Row Pub., 1973), 541.

31. Pollock, *Wilberforce*, 276.

Chapter Eight

1. A.P. Moore-Anderson, *Sir Robert Anderson* (London: Marshall, Morgan, and Scott, Ltd., 1947), 18–20.

2. Ibid.

3. Ibid., 42.

4. Ibid., 45.

5. Ibid., 41.

6. Major LeCaron, *Twenty-Five Years in the Secret Service* (London: n.p., n.d.), 25.

7. Moore-Anderson, *Sir Robert Anderson*, 54–55.

8. Ibid., 51.

9. Ibid., 63.

10. Ibid., 52.

11. Ibid., 39.

12. Ibid., 12.

13. Ibid., 72.

14. Ibid., 68.

15. Ibid., 68–70.

16. Ibid., 70–80.

Chapter Nine

1. I am indebted to Frank Vandenberg's *Abraham Kuyper* (Grand Rapids: William B. Eerdman's Publishing Co., 1960), the only complete biography in English, for most of the essential information.

2. Ibid., 11.

3. Ibid., 17.

4. Ibid., 21.

5. Ibid., 35.

6. Ibid., 33.

7. Ibid., 48.

8. Ibid., 47.

9. W. Stanford Reid, ed., *John Calvin's Influence in the Western World* (Grand Rapids, Mich.: Zondervan Publishing House, 1982), 115.

10. Ibid., 116.

11. G. Groen van Prinsterer, *Unbelief and Revolution, Lecture VIII* (Amsterdam: The Groen van Prinsterer Fund, 1975), 29f.

12. A full account of this tragedy is given in Otto Scott's *Robspierre: The Voice of Virtue* (New York: Mason and Lipscomb Pub., 1974).

13. Gary North, ed., *The Theology of Christian Resistance* (Tyler, Texas: Geneva Divinity School Press, 1983), 312.

14. Vandenberg, *Abraham Kuyper*, 65.

15. Ibid., 52.

16. Ibid., 58.

17. Ibid., 48.

18. Ibid., 68.

19. John Chamberlain, *The Roots of Capitalism* (Indianapolis: Liberty Press, 1976, originally pub. D. Van Nostrand Co., 1959), 70–71.

20. Robert A. Peterson, "Lessons in Liberty: The Dutch Republic, 1579-1750," *The Freeman* (July 1987): 259–264.

21. Gary DeMar, *God and Government* (Atlanta: American Vision Press, 1982), 12.

22. Vandenberg, *Abraham Kuyper*, 62–63.

23. Elmer Towns, ed., *A History of Religious Educators* (Grand Rapids: Baker Book House, 1975), 296.

24. Vandenberg, *Abraham Kuyper*, 144.

25. Ibid., 155.

26. Ibid., 192.

27. Otto Scott, *The Other End of the Lifeboat* (Chicago: Regnery Books, 1985), 24–25.

28. Vandenberg, *Abraham Kuyper*, 255.

29. Ibid., 255.

We welcome comments from our readers. Feel free to write to us at the following address:

Editorial Department
Huntington House Publishers
P.O. Box 53788
Lafayette, LA 70505

═══════════════════

More Good Books from Huntington House

New Gods for a New Age
by Richmond Odom

There is a new state religion in this country. The gods of this new religion are Man, Animals, and Earth. Its roots are deeply embedded in Hinduism and other Eastern religions. The author of *New Gods for a New Age* contends that this new religion has become entrenched in our public and political institutions and is being aggressively imposed on all of us. This humanistic-evolutionary world view has carried great destruction in its path which can be seen in college classrooms where Christianity is belittled, in the court-room where good is called evil and evil is called good, and in government where the self-interest of those who wield political power is served as opposed to the common good.

ISBN 1-56384-062-6 $9.99

Getting Out:
An Escape Manual for Abused Women
by Kathy L. Cawthon

Four million women are physically assaulted by their husbands, ex-husbands, and boyfriends each year. Of these millions of women, nearly 4,000 die. Kathy Cawthon, herself a former victim of abuse, uses her own experience and the expertise of law enforcement personnel to guide the reader through the process of escaping an abusive relationship. *Getting Out* also shows readers how they can become whole and healthy individuals instead of victims, giving them hope for a better life in the future.

ISBN 1-56384-093-6

Global Bondage
The U.N. Plan to Rule the World
by Cliff Kincaid

The U.N. is now openly laying plans for a World Government—to go along with its already functioning World Army. These plans include global taxation and an International Criminal Court that could prosecute American citizens. In *Global Bondage,* journalist Cliff Kincaid blows the lid off the United Nations. He warns that the move toward global government is gaining ground and that it will succeed if steps are not taken to stop it.

ISBN 1-56384-103-7 Tradepaper
ISBN 1-56384-109-6 Hardcover

One Man, One Woman, One Lifetime
An Argument for Moral Tradition
by Reuven Bulka

Lifestyles that have been recognized since antiquity as destructive and immoral are promoted today as acceptable choices. Rabbi Reuven Bulka challenges the notion that contemporary society has outgrown the need for moral guidelines. Using both scientific research and classical biblical precepts, he examines changing sexual mores and debunks the arguments offered by activists and the liberal media.

ISBN 1-56384-079-0 $7.99

The Extermination of Christianity-
A Tyranny of Consensus
by Paul Schenck with Robert L. Schenck

If you are a Christian, you might be shocked to discover that: Popular music, television, and motion pictures are consistently depicting you as a stooge, a hypocrite, a charlatan, a racist, an anti-Semite, or a con artist; you could be expelled from a public high school for giving Christian literature to a classmate; and you could be arrested and jailed for praying on school grounds. This book is a catalogue of anti-Christian propaganda—a record of persecution before it happens!

ISBN 1-56384-051-0 $9.99

Gays & Guns
The Case against Homosexuals
in the Military
by John Eidsmoe

The homosexual revolution seeks to overthrow the Laws of Nature. A Lieutenant Colonel in the United States Air Force Reserve, Dr. John Eidsmoe eloquently contends that admitting gays into the military would weaken the combat effectiveness of our armed forces. This cataclysmic step would also legitimize homosexuality, a lifestyle that most Americans know is wrong. While echoing Cicero's assertion that "a sense of what is right is common to all mankind," Eidsmoe rationally defends his belief. There are laws that govern the universe, he reminds us. Laws that compel the earth to rotate on its axis, laws that govern the economy; and so there is also a moral law that governs man's nature. The violation of this moral law is physically, emotionally and spiritually destructive. It is destructive to both the individual and to the community of which he is a member.

ISBN Trade Paper 1-56384-043-X $7.99
ISBN Hardcover 1-56384-046-4 $14.99

Conservative, American & Jewish—
I Wouldn't Have It Any Other Way
by Jacob Neusner

Neusner has fought on the front lines of the culture war and here writes reports about sectors of the battles. He has taken a consistent, conservative position in the academy, federal agencies in the humanities and the arts, and in the world of religion in general and Judaism in particular. Engaging, persuasive, controversial in the best sense, these essays set out to change minds and end up touching the hearts and souls of their readers.

ISBN 1-56384-048-0 $9.99

Political Correctness:
The Cloning of the American Mind
by David Thibodaux, Ph.D.

The author, a professor of literature at the University of Southwestern Louisiana, confronts head on the movement that is now being called Political Correctness. Political correctness, says Thibodaux, "is an umbrella under which advocates of civil rights, gay and lesbian rights, feminism, and environmental causes have gathered." To incur the wrath of these groups, one only has to disagree with them on political, moral, or social issues. To express traditionally Western concepts in universities today can result in not only ostracism, but even suspension. (According to a recent "McNeil-Lehrer News Hour" report, one student was suspended for discussing the reality of the moral law with an avowed homosexual. He was reinstated only after he apologized.)

ISBN 1-56384-026-X Trade Paper $9.99

Beyond Political Correctness:
Are There Limits to This Lunacy?
by David Thibodaux

Author of the best-selling *Political Correctness: The Cloning of the American Mind,* Dr. David Thibodaux now presents his long awaited sequel—*Beyond Political Correctness: Are There Limits to This Lunacy?* The politically correct movement has now moved beyond college campuses. The movement has succeeded in turning the educational system of this country into a system of indoctrination. Its effect on education was predictable: steadily declining scores on every conceivable test which measures student performance; and, increasing numbers of college freshmen who know a great deal about condoms, homosexuality, and abortion, but whose basic skills in language, math, and science are alarmingly deficient.

ISBN 1-56384-066-9 $9.99

The Assault: Liberalism's Attack on Religion, Freedom, and Democracy
by Dale A. Berryhill

In *The Liberal Contradiction,* Berryhill showed just how ludicrous it is when civil rights advocates are racists and feminists are sexists. Now he turns to much more disturbing phenomena, revisiting such issues as censorship, civil rights, gay rights, and political correctness in education and offering commentary and punishment, civil liberties, multiculturalism, and religious freedom. Fortunately, the American people are catching on to the hypocrisy. Still, the culture war is far from over.

ISBN 1-56384-077-4 $9.99

The Media Hates Conservatives: How It Controls the Flow of Information
by Dale A. Berryhill

Here is clear and powerful evidence that the liberal leaning news media brazenly attempted to influence the outcome of the election between President George Bush and Candidate Bill Clinton. Through a careful analysis of television and newspaper coverage, this book confirms a consistent pattern of liberal bias (even to the point of assisting the Clinton campaign). The major media outlets have taken sides in the culture war. Through bias, distortion, and the violation of professional standards, they have opposed the traditional values embraced by conservatives and most Americans, to the detriment of our country.

ISBN 1-56384-060-X $9.99

When the Wicked Seize a City
by Chuck & Donna McIlhenny with Frank York

A highly publicized lawsuit . . . a house fire-bombed in the night . . . the shatter of windows smashed by politically (and wickedly) motivated vandals cuts into the night . . . All because Chuck McIlhenny voiced God's condemnation of a behavior and life-style and protested the destruction of society that results from its practice. That behavior is homosexuality, and that life-style is the gay culture. This book explores: the rise of gay power and what it will mean if Christians do not organize and prepare for the battle, and homosexual attempts to have the American Psychiatric Association remove pedophilia from the list of mental illnesses (now they want homophobia declared a disorder).

ISBN 1-56384-024-3 $9.99

The Culture War in America
A Society in Chaos
by Bob Rosio

Without the strong moral foundation of the Judeo-Christian tradition to sustain us, America is fragmenting into a variety of pagan sects. Radical feminism, earth worship, occult activity, and out-and-out hedonism are just a few of the belief systems driving social policy today. Ironically, few seem to realize that this is the reason we are plagued by crime, divorce, drug addiction, and a failing education system. *The Culture War in America* shows how we can individually and collectively return America to the values on which it was founded.

ISBN 1-56384-097-9

Out of Control—
Who's Watching Our Child
Protection Agencies?
by Brenda Scott

This book of horror stories is true. The deplorable and unauthorized might of Child Protection Services is capable of reaching into and destroying any home in America. No matter how innocent and happy your family may be, you are one accusation away from disaster. Social workers are allowed to violate constitutional rights and often become judge, jury, and executioner. Innocent parents may appear on computer registers and be branded "child abuser" for life. Every year, it is estimated that over 1 million people are falsely accused of child abuse in this country. You could be next, says author and speaker Brenda Scott.

ISBN 1-56384-069-3 $9.99

Children No More:
How We Lost a Generation
by Brenda Scott

Child abuse, school yard crime, gangland murders, popular lyrics laced with death motifs, twisted couplings posing as love on MTV and daytime soap operas (both accessible by latch-key children), loving parents portrayed as the enemy, condom pushers, drug apologists, philandering leaders . . . is it any wonder heroes and role models are passe? The author grieves the loss of a generation but savors a hope that the next can be saved.

ISBN 1-56384-083-9

"Soft Porn" Plays Hardball
by Dr. Judith A. Reisman

With amazing clarity, the author demonstrates that pornography imposes on society a view of women and children that encourages violence and sexual abuse. As crimes against women and children increase to alarming proportions, it's of paramount importance that we recognize the cause of this violence. Pornography should be held accountable for the havoc it has wreaked in our homes and our country.

ISBN Trade Paper 0-910311-65-X $8.99
ISBN Hardcover 0-910311-92-7 $16.99

Kinsey, Sex and Fraud: The Indoctrination of a People
by Dr. Judith A. Reisman and Edward Eichel

Kinsey, Sex and Fraud describes the research of Alfred Kinsey which shaped Western society's beliefs and understanding of the nature of human sexuality. His unchallenged conclusions are taught at every level of education—elementary, high school, and college—and quoted in textbooks as undisputed truth. The authors clearly demonstrate that Kinsey's research involved illegal experimentations on several hundred children. The survey was carried out on a non-representative group of Americans, including disproportionately large numbers of sex offenders, prostitutes, prison inmates, and exhibitionists.

ISBN 0-910311-20-X $10.99

A Jewish Conservative
Looks at Pagan America
by Don Feder

With eloquence and insight that rival essayists of antiquity, Don Feder's pen finds his targets in the enemies of God, family, and American tradition and morality. Deftly . . . delightfully . . . the master allegorist and Titian with a typewriter brings clarity to the most complex sociological issues and invokes giggles and wry smiles from both followers and foes. Feder is Jewish to the core, and he finds in his Judaism no inconsistency with an American Judeo-Christian ethic. Questions of morality plague school administrators, district court judges, senators, congressmen, parents, and employers; they are wrestling for answers in a "changing world." Feder challenges this generation and directs inquirers to the original books of wisdom: the Torah and the Bible.

ISBN 1-56384-036-7 Trade Paper $9.99
ISBN 1-56384-037-5 Hardcover $19.99

A Call to Manhood:
In a Fatherless Society
by David E. Long

Western society is crumbling—from the collapse of the family...to our ailing economic system, from the scandals in the church...to the corruptions in the Halls of Congress, from the decline of business...to the pollution of Hollywood, everywhere, we see moral and societal decay. The reason, says author David Long, is that the vast majority of men in America have received tragically inadequate fathering, ranging from an ineffective father to no father at all. This book presents a refreshing vision and a realistic strategy for men to recapture their biblical masculinity.

ISBN 1-56384-047-2 $9.99

Circle of Death
Clinton's Climb to the Presidency
by Richmond Odom

When President Bill Clinton was governor of Arkansas during the '70s and '80s, the state was a hotbed of drug-smuggling and gun-running. In connection with these activities, a series of murders took place. More recently, several people closely associated with Bill Clinton have committed suicide or died under extremely questionable circumstances, including a former Clinton bodyguard who allegedly kept files on then-Governor Clinton's sexual liaisons and four members of Clinton's security team. Why have so many in Clinton's circle of power become part of this circle of death? Weigh the evidence, consider the facts, and arrive at your own conclusions.

ISBN 1-56384-089-8

The Blame Game
Why Society Persecutes Christians
by Lynn Stanley

As an increasing number of Americans recognize their right to traditional values and religious freedom, the liberal media increases its efforts to suppress these liberties. At the same time, liberal courts and organizations such as the NEA work to eliminate religion from American culture. In *The Blame Game*, Lynn Stanley exposes the groups attacking the constitutional rights of Americans to tradition and freedom of religion. Also, she explains what these factions fear from mainstream America and why they seek to destroy it through their un-American system of wretched moral relativism.

ISBN 1-56384-090-1

High-Voltage Christianity
Sparking the Spirit in the Church
by Dr. Michael L. Brown

Something unusual is happening in the church today. All around us we see signs of revival. Is true revival coming to America? Dr. Michael L. Brown examines the difference between counterfeit revival and genuine spiritual change, confronting both Hollywood-style sensationalism and spiritual slumber. Never has the subject of revival been so thoroughly, or passionately, considered.

ISBN 1-56384-088-X

Everyday Evangelism
Witnessing That Works
by Ray Comfort

This warm, funny, down-to-earth volume is filled with suggestions on how to reach out to others. Whether you're in a restaurant, at work, or even at the mall, there are many easy, effective and inoffensive ways to share your faith. As practical as it is entertaining, *Everyday Evangelism* is one book every Christian will enjoy—and refer to again and again.

ISBN 1-56384-091-X

Anyone Can Homeschool
How to Find What Works for You
by Terry Dorian, Ph.D., and Zan Peters Tyler

Honest, practical, and inspirational, *Anyone Can Homeschool* assesses the latest in homeschool curricula and confirms there are social as well as academic advantages to home education. Both veteran and novice homeschoolers will gain insight and up-to-date information from this important new book.

ISBN 1-56384-095-2

Do Angels Really Exist?
Separating Fact from Fantasy
by Dr. David O. Dykes

Have you ever seen an angel? Don't be too quick to answer "no." For most of us, angels evoke images of winged, white figures frolicking from one cloud to another. But, according to the Bible, angels are God's armored warriors, ready to protect His kingdom in heaven, as well as His beloved followers on earth. By citing dozens of fascinating angel encounters, the author presents evidence that angels roam the earth today, protecting and comforting God's people. You might be encountering angels without even knowing it.

ISBN 1-56384-105-3

System Shakedown
Taking Back Our Schools
by Darylann Whitemarsh

A twenty-one year veteran of the public schools addresses the issues of greatest concern in education today: Goals 2000, private and public school choice, outcome-based education, multicultural curricula, sex education, homeschooling, and much more. Honest and up-to-date, *System Shakedown* is essential reading for parents, community leaders, teachers, and anyone else who wants to get our schools back on track.

ISBN 1-56384-094-4

Order These Huntington House Books !

- *Anyone Can Homeschool*—Terry Dorian & Zan Peters Tyler 7.99
- *The Assault*—Dale A. Berryhill 9.99
- *Beyond Political Correctness*—David Thibodaux 9.99
- *The Best of* Human Events—Edited by James C. Roberts 34.95
- *Bleeding Hearts and Propaganda*—James R. Spencer 9.99
- *Can Families Survive in Pagan America?*—Samuel Dresner 15.99
- *Circle of Death*—Richmond Odom 10.99
- *Children No More*—Brenda Scott 12.99
- *Combat Ready*—Lynn Stanley 9.99
- *Conservative, American & Jewish*—Jacob Neusner 9.99
- *The Dark Side of Freemasonry*—Ed Decker 9.99
- *The Demonic Roots of Globalism*—Gary Kah 10.99
- *Do Angels Really Exist?*—David O. Dykes 9.99
- *En Route to Global Occupation*—Gary Kah 9.99
- *Everyday Evangelism*—Ray Comfort 10.99
- **Exposing the AIDS Scandal*—Dr. Paul Cameron 7.99/2.99
- *Freud's War with God*—Jack Wright, Jr. 7.99
- *Gays & Guns*—John Eidsmoe ....7.99/14.99 HB
- *Global Bondage*—Cliff Kincaid 10.99
- *Goddess Earth*—Samantha Smith 9.99
- *Health Begins in Him*—Terry Dorian 9.99
- *Heresy Hunters*—Jim Spencer 8.99
- *Hidden Dangers of the Rainbow*—Constance Cumbey 9.99
- *High-Voltage Christianity*—Michael Brown 10.99
- *High on Adventure*—Stephen Arrington 8.99
- *Homeless in America*—Jeremy Reynalds 9.99
- *How to Homeschool (Yes, You!)*—Julia Toto 3.99
- *Hungry for God*—Larry E. Myers 9.99
- *I Shot an Elephant in My Pajamas*—Morrie Ryskind w/ John Roberts 12.99
- **Inside the New Age Nightmare*—Randall Baer 9.99/2.99
- *A Jewish Conservative Looks at Pagan America*—Don Feder ....9.99/19.99 HB
- *Journey into Darkness*—Stephen Arrington 9.99
- *Kinsey, Sex and Fraud*—Dr. Judith A. Reisman &   Edward Eichel 11.99
- *The Liberal Contradiction*—Dale A. Berryhill 9.99
- *Legalized Gambling*—John Eidsmoe 7.99
- *The Media Hates Conservatives*—Dale A. Berryhill ....9.99/19.99 HB
- *New Gods for a New Age*—Richmond Odom 9.99
- *One Man, One Woman, One Lifetime*—Rabbi Reuven Bulka 7.99
- *Out of Control*—Brenda Scott ....9.99/19.99 HB
- *Outcome-Based Education*—Peg Luksik & Pamela Hoffecker 9.99
- *The Parched Soul of America*—Leslie Kay Hedger w/ Dave Reagan 10.99
- *Please Tell Me*—Tom McKenney 9.99
- *Political Correctness*—David Thibodaux 9.99
- *Resurrecting the Third Reich*—Richard Terrell 9.99
- *Revival: Its Principles and Personalities*—Winkie Pratney 10.99

*Available in Salt Series

Available at bookstores everywhere or order direct from:
Huntington House Publishers • P.O. Box 53788 • Lafayette, LA 70505
Send check/money order. For faster service use VISA/MASTERCARD.
Call toll-free 1-800-749-4009.
Add: Freight and handling, $3.50 for the first book ordered, and $.50 for
each additional book up to 5 books.